THE EXPANDING CHURCH

THE EXPANDING CHURCH

Spencer J. Palmer

Deseret Book Company
Salt Lake City, Utah
1978

Library of Congress Cataloging in Publication Data

Palmer, Spencer J
    The expanding church.

    Includes bibliographical references and index.
    1. Church Jesus Christ of Latter-day Saints—
Missions.
I. Title.
BX8661.P34   266'.9'33   78-26082
ISBN 0-87747-732-9

Based upon ancient and modern revelation, The Church of Jesus Christ of Latter-day Saints gladly teaches and declares the Christian doctrine that all men and women are brothers and sisters, not only by blood relationship from common mortal progenitors, but also as literal spirit children of an Eternal Father.

The great religious leaders of the world such as Mohammed, Confucius, and the Reformers, as well as philosophers including Socrates, Plato, and others, received a portion of God's light. Moral truths were given to them by God to enlighten whole nations and to bring a higher level of understanding to individuals.

The Hebrew prophets prepared the way for the coming of Jesus Christ, the promised Messiah, who should provide salvation for all mankind who believe in the gospel.

Consistent with these truths, we believe that God has given and will give to all peoples sufficient knowledge to help them on their way to eternal salvation, either in this life or in the life to come.

We also declare that the gospel of Jesus Christ, restored to his Church in our day, provides the only way to a mortal life of happiness and a fulness of joy forever. For those who have not received this gospel, the opportunity will come to them in the life hereafter if not in this life.

Our message therefore is one of special love and concern for the eternal welfare of all men and women, regardless of religious belief, race, or nationality, knowing that we are truly brothers and sisters because we are the sons and daughters of the same Eternal Father.

Statement of the First Presidency
February 15, 1978

CONTENTS

ACKNOWLEDGMENTS

This study of the momentous expansion of The Church of Jesus Christ of Latter-day Saints since the end of World War II stems back to the author's days as a Mormon chaplain in Asia during the early 1950s. This was when I first realized that Mormonism was on the threshold of becoming a world-embracing faith.

The process would take time, I realized, but along the way steps would be taken that could be delineated by the very people who were involved in the expansion. A few of those steps and some of those people might be introduced through their own descriptions of events they helped bring about or of the effects of these events on their lives. This collection of experiences, then, could be a sampling of the whole, a microcosm representing the universality of the Mormon message, a few accounts representing the many that might be recorded as the gospel of Jesus Christ continues its spread "to every nation, kindred, tongue, and people." (D&C 133:37.)

Thanks to the vision and mobility of living prophets, I have been inspired for many years at the prospect of a universal kingdom in the making, and of the critical importance of remembering and recording its history. But in an immediate sense, the idea for this book originated with Leonard J. Arrington, the Church Historian. I am sincerely grateful to him for his splendid example of scholarship and faith, and to his staff—Maureen Ursenbach Beecher, Davis Bitton, and James B. Allen—for their constructive review of the preliminary manuscript.

I would like to thank Jeffrey R. Holland, Martin B. Hickman, Ellis T. Rasmussen, and Charles D. Tate for reading early drafts and for being so consistently kind and helpful.

I deeply appreciate the assistance of Lyle R. Drake and Robert F. Norton; the editorial and typing assistance of John N. Drayton, Marla Whyte, Diane Morita, Eloise Fugal, and Estelle Farmer; the contributions of Joe J. Christensen and Neil J. Flinders in the preparation of the chapter on Church education; and the assistance of James O. Mason, Edward L. Soper, and Dean R. Zimmerman in preparing materials on the Church's health services. My sincere gratitude also goes to Elder Bruce R. McConkie for permission to reprint his address "To the Koreans, and All the People of Asia."

For many hours shared in recording, reviewing, and reflecting on their personal experiences, I am indebted to David M. Kennedy, a splendid friend and a worthy example; to the Karl Ringger family; to the Masao Watabe family; and to the Pablo Choc family. Their reflections are key contributions to this book, powerfully attesting to the internationalism of Mormonism and the universality of its appeal. I am also indebted to Soren N. Cox, Vaha'i Tonga, and R. Lanier Britsch for their important contributions.

For their help in obtaining the Pablo Choc story I am particularly indebted to Dr. Robert Blair for his generous introduction to the "Latin American Indian world" and to Mario Salazar for his translations of Pablo Choc's account and also his valuable insights into life among the people of Patzicia.

I wish also to express grateful acknowledgment to Eleanor Knowles, editor of Deseret Book Company, for her deft and skillful hand in trimming an originally lengthy and detailed manuscript into a simplified and more abbreviated book.

This volume is affectionately dedicated to my wife and, with her concurrence, to our beloved parents and children.

Of course, none of the persons named here would want to be held responsible for the interpretations or shortcomings of this work. And my attributions here are not intended to imply their endorsement of its contents. I humbly and happily reserve that responsibility to myself.

I

UNTO
EVERY
NATION,
KINDRED,
TONGUE,
& PEOPLE

1

UNTO EVERY NATION

There are ranges of mountains so vast — the Atlas, the Sierras, the Himalayas, the Andes, the Alps—that even when men have negotiated their passes and have begun to cross to the other side, they are not quite aware that they have, in truth, done so. And there is always uncertainty about the meaning of such experiences and how best to interpret new terrain that has opened to view.

In our time today, The Church of Jesus Christ of Latter-day Saints is crossing such a divide. The traditional geographically and culturally westernized church is rapidly becoming a global movement, widely dispersed and diversified. Mainstream Mormonism is no longer confined to one society in the western part of the United States, or even in an American setting. Now indeed it belongs to every nation, kindred, tongue, and people throughout the world. Particularly since the end of World War II, burgeoning growth and expansion have marked the course of the Church.

In each decade since the restoration of the Church in 1830, its leaders have reaffirmed that the gospel must be

taken to every country, race, and group. In 1901
Brigham Young, Jr., of the Council of the Twelve said,
"The eyes of the Twelve have been roaming over the
habitable globe, and they have looked upon Turkey,
Austria, Russia and especially South America. . . . We
have felt and do now feel that it is our duty . . . to go
forth . . . to the nations of the earth to proclaim the
gospel . . . when the spirit indicates the time and place."
(*Conference Report,* October 1901, p. 66.)

Forty-four years later, in the Church's semiannual
conference in October 1945, President George Albert
Smith concluded:

> It will not be long until the servants of the Lord will go again to
> the nations of the earth in great numbers. . . . We must preach the
> gospel to the South American countries which we have scarcely
> touched. We must preach the gospel to every African section that we
> haven't been in yet. We must preach the gospel to Asia. And I might
> go one step further and say in all parts of the world where we have
> not yet been permitted to go. I look upon Russia as one of the most
> fruitful fields for the teaching of the gospel. . . . Our most important
> obligation is to divide with our Father's children all those funda-
> mental truths known as the Gospel of Jesus Christ. . . . I have
> traveled in many lands and climes, and wherever I have gone I have
> found good people, sons and daughters of the living God who are
> waiting for the gospel of Jesus Christ, and there are thousands,
> hundreds of thousands, millions of them, who would be accepting
> the truth if they only knew what we know.

The application of these beliefs is seen in the beginning of missionary work in this dispensation. Shortly
after the gospel was restored, missionaries were sent to
various parts of the United States and into Canada. In a
time of hardship in Kirtland, Ohio, Joseph Smith sent
missionaries to Great Britain "to save the Church." (*History of the Church* 3:1-4.) Missionaries were sent from
Nauvoo, Illinois, to Australia, Ireland, and India in
1840; to South America and the West Indies in 1841;
and to Polynesia, Germany, and Russia in 1843. Within
thirty years after the Church was organized, eight formal
missions had been established: British, Society Islands,
Australian, East Indian, Maltese, Gilbralter, German,
and South African.

Since World War II, the responsibility for teaching the gospel has pressed even more heavily upon the Church. Many doors to missionary work have opened only recently. Wars in Japan and Korea introduced to those countries many Americans, and with them the gospel, initially through Latter-day Saint servicemen and later through missionaries sent to assist the ser-vicemen's converts. Elder Gordon B. Hinckley of the Council of the Twelve, speaking in the context of the war then waging in Vietnam, stated in 1968:

> I seek . . . to call your attention to that silver thread, small but radiant with hope, shining through the dark tapestry of war--namely, the establishment of a bridgehead, small and frail now; but which somehow under the mysterious ways of God, will be strengthened, and from which someday shall spring forth a great work affecting for good the lives of large numbers of our Father's children who live in that part of the world. Of that I have certain faith.
>
> I have seen a prototype of what will happen as I have witnessed the development of this work in others of the ancient nations of Asia--in Korea, in Taiwan, in Okinawa, in the Philippines, and in Japan. . . .
>
> This marvelous membership is the sweet fruit of seed once planted in dark years of war and in the troubled days immediately following, when good men of the priesthood, both civilian and military, through the example of their lives and the inspiration of their precepts, laid a foundation on which a great work has been established. (CR, April 1968, p. 24.)

The great work continues to grow--and with it the membership of the Church worldwide. Addressing the Latter-day Saints of Mexico and Central America at an area conference in 1972, President Harold B. Lee stated, "The greatest problem in the Church today is the problem of growth." In a meeting of priesthood leaders in Salt Lake City on December 6, 1975, President Spencer W. Kimball likewise concluded: "Our problem is big-ness. Our greatest problem today is how to take care of the flood of people who are now joining the Church."

The years since David O. McKay became president of the Church in 1951 have witnessed unprecedented growth and change. In that time the membership has more than tripled, increasing from 1,147,570 in 1951 to over four million by April 1978. The number of full-time missions increased from 43 in 1951 to 157 by the end of 1977. The number of stakes more than quadrupled: 191 in 1951, and 885 at the end of 1977.

Although recent growth as a whole has been extraordinary, the international expansion is of even greater significance. In 1951, only 8.1 percent of the total Church membership resided outside the United States; by 1978 the figure was approaching 25 percent. Latin America and Asia have been the areas of most rapid growth. In just one weekend in September 1976, Elder Howard W. Hunter of the Council of the Twelve, acting under the direction of the First Presidency, organized sixteen stakes in the Mexico City area alone.

The first stake outside North America and Hawaii was established in Auckland, New Zealand, in 1958. Since 1971 over half the stakes created have been outside the United States. In addition to temples erected in Switzerland (1955), New Zealand (1958), England (1958), and Brazil (1978), plans have been announced for temples in Japan, Mexico, Samoa, and Seattle, as well as a new one in Salt Lake County.

Church membership has been increasing at a faster rate than world population. Whereas Church membership increased 196 percent between 1951 and 1975, world population grew 57 percent during the same years. The ratio of Latter-day Saints to the total non-Mormon world population has also improved remarkably. In 1951 it was 1 to 2,069; by the end of 1975 it was 1 to 1,103.

The stone cut without hands is now visibly rolling forth with ever-increasing momentum, and this bodes a host of new challenges and changes for the Church. In an address of extraordinary boldness at a seminar for Regional Representatives in April 1974, President Kimball declared that Mormon congregations must be established in Ireland, Russia, North Korea, Mongolia, Yugoslavia, India, Cambodia, Arab lands, and all other places where the spread of the Church has thus far been delayed. He stated that the Lord will prepare the way, new bridges will be built, doors will be opened, and resources will be furnished only as members of the Church lengthen their stride, enlarge their vision, increase their faith, and become better prepared in knowledge, experience, and understanding of lands and peoples who have not previously been reached by the Church. How will this be accomplished? President Kimball specified some basic objectives for the Church, stressing that whether by means of unexpected wars and revolutions, the aid of friendly government officials, the assistance of influential Latter-day Saints, the efforts of servicemen, scholars, businessmen, and diplomats, an increase in the missionary force, or by any other means, the kingdom of God will yet spread among all peoples of the earth. (*Ensign,* October 1974, pp. 2-14.)

The same goals were reiterated even more forcefully at a seminar for Regional Representatives September 29, 1978, when President Kimball stated:

> We have an obligation, a duty, a divine commission to preach the gospel in every nation and to every creature. . . . We feel that the Spirit of the Lord is brooding over the nations to prepare the way for the preaching of the gospel.
>
> Some political events have a bearing upon the spread of the truth. It seems as though the Lord is moving upon the affairs of men and nations to hasten their day of readiness when leaders will permit the elect among them to receive the gospel of Jesus Christ and when the gospel will be preached "for a witness" among all nations. Much of the technology for telling the truths of the gospel seems to be in place, but we seem tardy as a people in availing ourselves of it. Technology and developments in transportation have made the world smaller, but it is still a big world so far as numbers of people are concerned when we think of nations like China, the Soviet Union, India, the whole continent of Africa, and our Arab brothers and sisters—hundreds of millions of our Father's children.
>
> Let us fellowship the students from all nations as they come to our land, so that we, above all other people, treat them as brothers and sisters in true friendship whether or not they are interested in the gospel. None of our Father in heaven's children are foreign to him, and this is his work. In the light of the gospel, they are "no more strangers and foreigners." (Ephesians 2:19.) . . .
>
> We have had a great increase in our missionary effort, for which we are grateful. We've created new missions and divided old ones; we've more than doubled our missionary force and we hope soon to

double it again. The Church and its members have begun to
respond faithfully to that commandment, "Go ye therefore," but . . .
we must stress the other part of the verse emphasizing *where* we must
go. The answer lies in our obligation to "teach all nations." . . . We
can bring the gospel with its healing balm and its powerful programs to countless numbers, not only to introduce the gospel to
them, but to show them in our communities how we live and how
they can live and better their lives. We have hardly scratched the
surface. . . .

. . . there seems to be a great movement afoot in many nations to
prepare people for the further light and knowledge that only we can
give them. The Lord by his Spirit is preparing people for the day
when the gospel will be taught them in plainness. We must be ready.

In response to the need for improved communication
in missionary work, the first Language Training Mission
was established in December 1961. Since that date more
than forty-five thousand missionaries have received specialized language training prior to entering their fields of
labor. All of the language training activities have now
been consolidated at a single location, in Provo, Utah
(buildings at Ricks College in Idaho and at Church
College of Hawaii, now Brigham Young University—
Hawaii Campus were previously used, as well as those in
Provo), and by fall of 1978 the "LTM," newly renamed
the Missionary Training Center, had facilities for some
three thousand missionaries. The program was originally
started for a group of missionaries going to Mexico; today three dozen languages are taught, including such
unusual ones as Afrikaans, Farsi (Persian), Serbo-
Croatian (Yugoslavian), and Icelandic.

Another significant development has been the calling
of General Authorities from widespread areas of the
world—Elder Adney Y. Komatsu, an American of
Japanese descent; Elder Charles A. Didier of Belgium;
Elder George P. Lee, an American Indian; Elder Jacob
deJager of the Netherlands; Elder Yoshihiko Kikuchi of
Japan; and Elder Derek H. Cuthbert of England.

The rapid growth of the Church has brought with it
problems of communication, building unity and brotherhood, training new leaders in farflung missions and
stakes, and administration of a worldwide church. One

effort to help solve these problems has been the appointment of Regional Representatives and, wherever possible, of mission presidents from these widespread areas.
The Quorum of the Seventy was organized in 1975 and
expanded to include all former Assistants to the Twelve
plus many new members, all of whom have General Authority status. The quorum will eventually be filled to its
capacity of seventy, and additional quorums may be
added as the Church and the missionary program
expand in the future.

As missionaries and other Church emissaries go to
new lands, in addition to problems in speaking new
tongues and providing accurate printed translations of
scripture and of instructions from Church headquarters,
they often also face problems of intercultural awareness.
To help solve these problems, Brigham Young
University established a Language Research Center in
1970. A Translation Sciences Institute is also being
developed at BYU for the development of computerized
translations of scriptures and other materials.

Church expansion into non-Western areas of the
world raises new questions regarding local cultures and
absolute truth. Latter-day Saints teach that the Church
seeks to embrace the beautiful and the true wherever
they may be found. Jesus Christ is the Light and the Life
of the Mormon faith, the universal Truth. And since
"neither is there salvation in any other; for there is none
other name under heaven given among men, whereby
we must be saved" (Acts 4:12), he is the Savior of all
mankind.

But Latter-day Saints live in a culturally diversified
world. They receive truth from the vantage point of
their own cultural and religious being, according to their
own language, values, customs, and ways of thinking.
Thus there is often distinction made between Christ and
cultures, the universal and the particular, value and history, the spiritual and the temporal, the absolute and the
situational, the divine and the human.

With all these considerations in mind, what precisely
is the relationship of the restored gospel to the cultures of

mankind? Is human culture enemy or friend? What is
the relationship of Mormonism to the great non-
Christian faiths? What about differences? And, much
more difficult to identify and evaluate, what about religious resemblances and parallels?

Each time different ways of life come together, they
run the risk of losing some of their original features.
Human organizations and traditions often become sub-
versive of gospel standards. Local cultures can adulterate
truth and lead to sin, fragmentation, and apostasy.

Yet, in Mormon belief, the gospel is congruent with
specific human values and traditions. Indeed, God has
expressed his mind and will to men within a variety of
cultural systems. There is an influence that emanates
from God that is not confined to selected nations, races,
or groups. All men share in an inheritance of divine
light. Christ himself is the light of the world, and even
those who have never heard of him are granted his spirit
and light.

In the teachings of latter-day scriptures, God
operates among his children in all nations. In the Book
of Mormon, Alma affirms that the Lord grants unto all
nations, of their own nation and tongue, to teach in
wisdom his word, all that he sees fit that they should
have. (Alma 29:8.)

The living prophet and president of the Church com-
municates God's will to those within the Church and to
all who are prepared and willing to listen. In addition to
the prophet, God may employ other spokesmen. B.H.
Roberts explained, "It is nowhere held that this man
[the living prophet] is the only instrumentality through
which God may communicate his mind and will to the
world." (B.H. Roberts, *Defense of the Faith and the Saints*
[Salt Lake City: The Deseret News, 1907], 1:514.)

All who seek God are entitled to further light and
knowledge, regardless of historical or cultural setting.
Elder John A. Widtsoe wrote: "Spiritual outreachings
are not peculiar to one country. Instead, in every land
men have sought the gifts of the spirit. . . . Men have
arisen in every land, who have tried to formulate the

way to happiness, for the benefit of themselves and their fellow men. . . . The religions of Egypt, China, India, and Persia, are examples." (*Gospel Interpretations* [Salt Lake City: Bookcraft, 1947], 2:216.)

According to Elder Orson F. Whitney, such religious leaders as Mahavira, Mohammed, and Confucius were inspired men:

> [God] is using not only his covenant people, but other peoples as well, to consummate a work, stupendous, magnificent, and altogether too arduous for this little handful of Saints to accomplish by and of themselves. . . . All down the ages men bearing the authority of the Holy Priesthood—patriarchs, prophets, apostles and others, have officiated in the name of the Lord, doing the things that he required of them; and outside the pale of their activities other good and great men, not bearing the Priesthood, but possessing profundity of thought, great wisdom, and a desire to uplift their fellows, have been sent by the Almighty into many nations to give them, not the fulness of the Gospel, but that portion of truth that they were able to receive and wisely use. Such men as Confucius, the Chinese philosopher; Zoroaster, the Persian sage; Gautama or Buddha, of the Hindus; Socrates and Plato, of the Greeks; these all had some of the light that is universally diffused, and concerning which we have this day heard. They were servants of the Lord in a lesser sense, and were sent to those pagan or heathen nations to give them the measure of truth that a wise Providence had allotted to them.
>
> And not only teachers—not poets and philosophers alone; but inventors, discoverers, warriors, statesmen, rulers, *et al.* These also have been used from the beginning to help along the Lord's work—mighty auxiliaries in the hands of an Almighty God, carrying out his purposes, consciously or unconsciously. (*CR*, April 1921, pp. 32-33.)

The scriptures suggest that through the light of Christ the sacred texts of Islam, Hinduism, Buddhism, Taoism, Confucianism, and Shinto may well have within them inspired and inspirational principles, and that the inhabitants of lands where these ideologies prevail will be judged by God in accordance with their individual willingness to abide by them, at least until a fulness of the gospel has been provided.

Although the spirit and power of Christ are manifest in all cultures, the founders and teachers of the great religions of the world have not received the gift of the

Holy Ghost or the keys of the holy priesthood. They have not received the celestial endowments of the temples of God, nor do they possess divine authority to perform the sanctifying ordinances of baptism and celestial marriage. Therefore, from the Latter-day Saint viewpoint, Buddha might have been the light of Asia, but he could not be the Light of the world; he was neither appointed nor empowered to that Messiahship. Likewise, Mohammed was an inspired instrument in the hands of God, but he was called to perform a special mission, at a special time, among a people who were in special need. Theirs were preparatory offices of great importance in the hand-dealings of God with mankind.

In the efforts of the Church to preserve truth, to build Zion and brotherhood among the Saints worldwide, and to reach out into the unknown, members are seeking to understand one another and achieve unity in what is essentially a world of many cultures. The Saints seek truth wherever it may be found, whether on Christian or "heathen" ground.

Thus there is a growing awareness in the Church today of the need to distinguish between misunderstandings that are based upon differences between gospel truths and local traditions and those that are based upon differences between the cultures involved. Moreover, there are traditions, customs, and beliefs about which the revelations of the Lord are silent—such preferences as language, food, art and architecture, wearing apparel, dance, music, and literature. These customs have no particular bearing on the capacity of an individual to gain the celestial kingdom; and so, in this day of the worldwide church, Latter-day Saints are attempting to become more aware of the need to accept and appreciate such distinctions. They must learn how to ensure that uncompromising truth is preserved without doing violence to foreign cultures simply because of the different cultural preferences of other peoples. And they are becoming aware of the difference between conversion to Christ and conversion to a culture.

In the New Testament, Peter's experience with Cornelius illustrates this point. The Lord was able to convince Peter that the gospel is not culturebound, but he did so in terms of a Hebrew language and culture Peter would understand. (Acts 10.) Peter was a Jew, and, though a Christian, he understood Christianity according to Hebrew patterns. But it was his task to carry the revelation that he had received in Hebrew dress, and to which he had responded in Hebrew terms, to Cornelius, a Roman and a member of another culture.

Since Peter's cultural heritage—as with that of all men—had a tendency to confine him to certain directions of thought and action, he assumed that only Hebrew culture was a suitable vehicle of God's communication. But the Lord admonished him in a Hebrew way, by commanding him in a vision to kill and eat animals that Judaism had pronounced unclean. He also convinced Peter that at least one Roman person, whom Peter had hitherto regarded as "unclean," was acceptable to God. Peter testified of his newfound discovery, saying, "Of a truth I perceive that God is no respecter of persons; but in every nation he that feareth him, and worketh righteousness, is accepted by him." (Acts 10:34-35.)

A considerable number of Cornelius's relatives and friends responded to the universal message delivered by Peter, and they received from God the confirmation that they had been accepted by him without their having first to become Jews.

The gospel of Jesus Christ enables men to see the true center of their lives in the life, power, and standards of the Savior, instead of in their cultures. Cultural precepts and teachings must be measured by the standard of revealed gospel truths. Thus God's design calls for a new creation from within national life, but not one that is limited even to the noblest that is available within one's own culture. New commitments to Christ and the principles and ordinances of his gospel often require radical changes and revolutionary displacements in the lives of members. Indeed, Brigham Young prophesied, "The gospel will revolutionize the whole world of mankind." (*Journal of Discourses* 24:60.) President Harold B. Lee expressed this idea even more explicitly: "The Church of Jesus Christ of Latter-day Saints stands today as it has always stood, as a continuing revolution against the norms of a society that fall below the standards of the gospel." (*Youth and the Church* [Deseret News Press, 1970], p. 7.)

Although carrying the gospel throughout the world in a multitude of languages is a monumental task, an even greater task must be accomplished before the coming of Christ: the establishing of congregations worldwide. Nephi, the Book of Mormon prophet, saw in vision events of the latter days preceding the second coming: "I beheld that the Church of the Lamb, who were the saints of God, were also upon all the face of the earth." (1 Nephi 14:12.) President Joseph Fielding Smith reiterated this concept in the British area conference in 1971 when he declared: ". . . not only shall we preach the gospel in every nation before the second coming of the Son of Man, but we shall make converts and establish congregations of Saints among them."

This development is sometimes called the gathering of Israel and at other times the establishment of Zion. Among Latter-day Saints today it consists of converts and members joining together in the true church and worshiping God in their own lands. Zion is no longer one physical axis; rather, it is many local congregations situated throughout the earth. In this era of transition, the law of gathering recognizes that there are many lands of promise, many lands of special inheritance, many lands of Zion. It also includes a call to join forces with one's own kindred in building up Zion communities within one's own land. National and regional groups should happily preserve their own identities within the Church, for in a final sense, particular peoples will yet receive special assignments and blessings from God.

With a focus on Zion communities worldwide, the question is no longer simply the Anglo-Americans' "How shall we instruct the foreign nations?"--nor even

"How will we be received?" Now the question is, "What does the gospel mean to me as an Indonesian (or Italian, Brazilian, or Japanese)?"

Other Church members are learning to see the gospel through the eyes of converts in every corner of the globe. What impact does the gospel have in the life of a native convert in France, Thailand, or Tonga? What happens to his self-esteem? What about his perception of neighbors in his own country? What is his perception of Americans and of American Latter-day Saints? How do the answers to these questions affect his adjustment to full participation in the Church? Do those answers enhance Church influence—or influence the Church?

As congregations are established worldwide, priesthood and auxiliary organizations are called upon to respond to individual needs—to help the Saints realize their full potential physically, intellectually, socially, and economically, as well as spiritually. As the apostle James admonished, "If a brother or sister be naked, and destitute of daily food, And one of you say unto them, Depart in peace, be ye warmed and filled; notwithstanding ye give them not those things which are needful to the body; what doth it profit?" (James 2:15-16.) In the Book of Mormon, King Benjamin taught that we are required to "succor those that stand in need" of our substance, that they do not cry out for help in vain. (Mosiah 4:15-19.) That responsibility of caring for temporal, social, and educational needs is part of the gospel plan and must now be met among Latter-day Saints in far-flung lands.

The response is forthcoming. According to a report prepared by the Church Educational System in late 1977, Church education has now reached out to fifty-five countries in the world. Enrollment now includes more than 33,000 students in LDS institutions of higher learning, and some 300,000 high school and college students in seminaries and institutes of religion.

Religious education has been expanded into the Cook Islands, Gilbert Islands, New Hebrides, and the outer islands of Tahiti, and plans have been laid to introduce the program in Indonesia and Thailand. A literacy program, first introduced in Bolivia in mid-1972, has been expanded to include the teaching of such basic skills as reading, writing, and arithmetic in other areas of the world, including the Cakchiquel language of Guatemala. Another recent development, of incalculable temporal benefit to members in Latin America, the Pacific, and East Asia, has been the establishment of scholarship funds to assist the poor or the disadvantaged.

By means of gospel-tempered training, Latter-day Saint students throughout the world are now being prepared with leadership skills by which they can perpetuate and further strengthen Church as well as non-Church educational opportunities for themselves and for others. These young people also greatly strengthen local congregations, leading Elder Howard W. Hunter to observe in 1971, "The growth of the Church has been the highest in the areas where we have established schools." (*BYU Studies,* Autumn 1971, p. 83.)

Similarly the Health Services program of the Church has sought to adapt itself to the changing needs of the membership. The Church has divested itself of its hospitals in Utah and Idaho because they served too limited a percentage of the membership, and has accelerated its efforts to meet the health needs of members worldwide.

The commission to carry the gospel unto every nation, kindred, tongue, and people carries with it a whole range of complex challenges. But the Church is negotiating the passes, and many have already crossed the divide. New nations, new cultures, new languages, new people—wherever we are, we have begun to grapple with the challenges of this vast terrain.

2

EACH IN HIS OWN TONGUE

An explicit objective of the Church is to lift "the curse of Babel" and to overcome the barriers of language that have heretofore inhibited the spread of the gospel in the earth. To this end, members have repeatedly been admonished to study foreign languages and to seek the gifts of the Spirit, including the gift of tongues, that the revelations of God might be widely disseminated.

Joseph Smith said that the gift of tongues was not for a sign, but to bring about understanding among peoples of different languages and tongues. (*History of the Church* [*HC*] 3:379.) "When devout men from every nation shall assemble to hear the things of God," he said, "let the Elders preach to them in their own tongue, whether it is German, Spanish or Irish, or any other, and let those interpret who understand the language, in their own mother tongue, and this is what the Apostle meant in 1 Corinthians 14:27." (*HC* 4:486.)

President Joseph F. Smith similarly instructed Latter-day Saints who were called to labor as missionaries where foreign languages are spoken: "Let them pray to God to give them knowledge by the gift of His Holy

Spirit as well as by study. There is where the gift of
tongues comes in, and where it is useful." (*Liahona*
12:776.)

We know we must make the scriptures available in
every tongue, in fulfillment of Jeremiah's admonition
that all the earth must hear the word of the Lord
(Jeremiah 22:29), and the Lord's word in our own day
that all men shall hear the fulness of the gospel in their
own tongue and language (D&C 90:10-11). However,
the complexity of fulfilling these commandments becomes apparent when we attempt to answer the simple
question, What is a language? In some areas of the
world, local government decree has given language
status to a dialect. In other areas, what are really distinct
languages have been regarded as mere dialects, such as
in the many so-called dialects of Chinese (Hakka, Chihli,
Swatow, etc.). In nearly all countries one's mother
tongue is an ambiguous combination of language and
local dialects that tend to differentiate in subtle but
substantial ways.

It is generally believed there are in the world thirteen
languages with at least fifty million users each. Another
hundred languages are spoken by at least one million
each, many of which are comparatively little known.
And there are many others that have not yet been written down. V. Lynn Tyler of the Language Research
Center at Brigham Young University pointed out, in a
1974 symposium on intercultural communication and
language concerns, that earlier estimates of 3,000 languages in the world must now be revised; recent studies
had identified at least 5,687 separate languages worldwide, including 1,956 in Asia; 1,741 in Africa; 1,039 in
the Pacific; 863 in the Americas; 46 in Europe; and 42 in
the Middle East.

Simply to identify all the languages spoken and written on earth is an enormous challenge. But for members
of the restored church to be able to speak, read, and
write all these tongues in such a way that those who
listen and respond will fully grasp and understand the
gospel message—that is perhaps the supreme task facing

the Church in the days ahead. It will require great inspiration and study; it will also require relentless, exact-
ing, and indefatigable translation work. Although much
has already been done, much remains.

By the end of 1970 the entire Bible had been translated and published in 249 languages and the New
Testament in an additional 329 languages, while individual books of the Bible had been produced in 853
other languages and dialects. These 1,431 languages into
which at least part of the Bible has been translated,
published, and distributed represent some 97 percent of
the world's population. This may well indicate, as the
United Bible Society claims, that the translation of the
Bible is one of the great accomplishments in communication in the history of the world. (Eugene A. Nida, *The
Book of 1,000 Tongues* [London: United Bible Society,
1971].)

The situation regarding the translation of the Book
of Mormon as well as the other standard works of the
Restoration is decidedly less extensive and complete. By
mid-1976 the Book of Mormon had been translated into
and published in only 25 major languages. It was being
prepared for publication in eight other languages, and
translated in fifteen others. (For current data, see the
Church Almanac, published annually by the *Church News*.)
In addition, portions of the Book of Mormon were either
available on cassette tapes or were scheduled for translation in the near future in eight Indian languages. The
Doctrine and Covenants and Pearl of Great Price have
been translated into even fewer languages.

Yet the demand for scriptures and for the word of
the living prophets has continued to keep pace with the
accelerating growth of the Church since World War II.
This in part is what gave rise in 1965 to the organization
of the Church's Translation Services Department, which
has been given major responsibility for finding ways to
bring to pass the Prophet Joseph Smith's prophecy that
"every man shall hear the fulness of the gospel in his
own tongue, and in his own language."

Although it can be said that rapid Church growth

has increased the need for translation services, the reverse may also be true: the rapid growth of stakes in non-English-speaking areas since 1965 may have been made possible in part by a new wealth of translated materials produced under the direction of that department. Both the output and the impact have been amazing. Distribution centers have been established to supply the needs of missionaries and members in such far-flung areas as Manchester, England; Auckland, New Zealand; Frankfurt, Germany; Copenhagen, Denmark; Mexico City, Mexico; Sao Paulo, Brazil; Buenos Aires, Argentina; Papeete, Tahiti; Apia, Samoa; Nuku'alofa, Tonga; Tokyo, Japan; Hong Kong; Seoul, Korea; Taipei, Taiwan; and Manila, the Philippines.

Translation Services has been given two basic tasks: (1) to make it possible for millions of people to learn the truths of the gospel in their own language, and (2) to meet the needs of a greatly expanded membership. The first deals primarily with missionary work; the second, with the growing administrative and operational concerns. The first is concerned with tracts, posters, and aids for open houses and proselyting work, as well as some one million copies of the Book of Mormon per year. The second is concerned with lesson manuals, handbooks, forms, and other supplies needed in stakes, wards, and branches.

Ten specific assignments have been given to the Translation Services Department:*

1. Scriptures and temple ceremony. It is estimated that if the Book of Mormon were published in approximately one hundred languages, it could be read by 90 percent of the world's population. Under the direction of the Church's temple committee, Translation Services has updated all translations of the temple ceremony to bring them in harmony with the original En-

---

*The author is grateful to John E. Carr and Justus Ernst of the Translation Services Department for supplying this information, much of which was given in an audiovisual presentation to General Authorities in the summer of 1975.

glish version, and has aided in the synchronization of the foreign-language sound tracks of the temple film.

2. Missionary discussions and tracts.

3. Stake conference, regional meeting, and other leadership materials. These, of course, are of special concern to the General Authorities as they visit the stakes, and they are vital to the growing problem of leadership training and development among new converts.

4. Motion pictures, filmstrips, and visual aids. These important materials must be synchronized into various languages, and subtitles must be provided where necessary.

5. Curricula, for the priesthood and the auxiliary organizations.

6. Hardbound books.

7. International magazines. Articles and other features appearing in the *Ensign*, *New Era*, and *Friend* are selected each month for translation and publication in international magazines currently published in sixteen languages.

8. Forms, reports, and music.

9. Correspondence. All written inquiries and communications received at Church headquarters in a non-English language are customarily forwarded to Translation Services for translation. Patriarchal blessings must be translated when the patriarch speaks a different language from that spoken by the recipient of the blessing.

10. Interpreting. Interpreters are provided for general and area conferences. Several rows in the Salt Lake Tabernacle are equipped with headphone jacks and dials so listeners can hear the interpretation of general conference proceedings in their native language.

In the past translations of scriptures and other materials were done primarily by missionaries, with some assistance by native-speaking persons. In recent years this procedure has been changed; today most translators work in their native language with English as a second language. Thus we find Asians, Latin Americans, and

Europeans translating into their native languages, sometimes with English-speaking missionaries acting as consultants. This has produced a dramatic swing toward decentralization in a very short time.

Computers have played a great part in these developments. The Translation Sciences Institute at Brigham Young University has prepared a computer program that lists words occurring in the standard works in each context in which they appear. The result is a voluminous listing of words known as a "Key-Word-in-Context" list. This has proved valuable in locating parallel phrases throughout the standard works so they can be translated consistently wherever they appear.

The institute has also become involved in construction of computerized dictionaries to assist Translation Services. This system allows a Church translator to largely-replace his desk dictionary with a computer terminal on which he can instantly check all meanings of a word. He simply types the word on his computer terminal, and a list of meanings appears on the screen. When he types an appropriate command on the terminal, the Spanish, French, Portuguese, German, or Chinese equivalents for any of these meanings can also be retrieved.

In preparing programs for the computers, it has become apparent that the most useful kind of dictionary for Church translators is not one that contains every word in the English language, but special words and terms of peculiar need for the translators. Thus the preparation of non-English equivalents for terms such as "priesthood," "special interests," and "Holy Ghost" has been given priority.

Closely related to this problem is one related to inconsistency of translations. Sometimes identical phrases that are found in more than one place in a given book of scripture have been translated differently by the same translator. One way in which computers can help solve this problem is to have all meanings of a given term put into the computer for retrieval and recall, with parallel English word meanings, foreign-word equivalents, and their variant meanings. Such computerized dictionaries can also be planned to reflect the dialects and colloquialisms of English spoken by those who originate most of the materials translated and published by the Church.

With these marvelous new developments, some of which have already been brought to fruition and some of which are still in the planning and developmental stages, the Church is coming ever closer to its goal of making the gospel available in other tongues and languages. Much work remains to be done, but great strides are being made as modern technology combines with inspired direction to help ensure that all the earth will one day hear the word of the Lord.

3

BUILDING
BROTHERHOOD

The blessings conferred upon Abraham were very great. They were later transmitted to his posterity. Because of these special blessings, the descendants of Israel have become known as a chosen people, and a concern for identification with this lineage is of great importance in the Church today.*

But in Mormon belief, the house of Israel is not confined to a small group of races or nations. The children of Abraham have been scattered upon all the face of the earth. Israel dwells upon the islands of the sea, in the countries and nations of Europe, in Africa, among the peoples of Mexico, Central America, and South America, and in the kingdoms and lands of Asia. The array of physical evidence attesting to this worldwide dispersion of Israel is clearly supported by scripture and by the living leaders of the Church. Thus, the lineage of Israel is not narrowly confined; and what is

*For example, the office of patriarch is a lineal office (D&C 107:39-40); the office of Presiding Bishop may be lineal also (D&C 107:76). Patriarchs are given specific instructions to declare the lineage of each recipient of a patriarchal blessing.

more, the blessings upon Abraham are universal in scope.

Although there are those on earth who do not literally and directly descend from Abraham, such people have not been treated intolerantly by God. He has not granted special blessings to Israelites without providing a way whereby gentiles (that is, non-Israelites in blood) may also receive those blessings or an opportunity to be worthy of them. There are ample instances of this in the scriptures. Cyrus, God's "anointed" king of Persia (Isaiah 45:1), and Ahasuerus, Esther's husband (Esther 2:17), were probably Zoroastrians whom the Lord used to further his purposes.

Many other gentiles were favored of Jehovah only because they were righteous and God-fearing men. These included Namaan, the leper healed by Elisha (2 Kings 5); the centurion whose servant was healed by Christ (Matthew 8:5-10); Cornelius, the Roman who was baptized by Peter (Acts 10); and the Ethiopian baptized by Philip (Acts 8:27-39).

The apostle Paul was specifically chosen to take the gospel to the gentiles. He championed the cause of gentile conversion to Christianity without adoption of Jewish practices. His letters to gentile Christians reveal his view of the inclusiveness of the church and its message; they also emphasize the doctrine that faithful gentiles who join the church are thereby adopted into the house of Israel. (Ephesians 3:5-6; Romans 10:12-13; Joseph Smith, *HC* 2:3, 380.)

In a realistic sense, the true lineage of Abraham is those who receive the gospel; and, according to Elder John A. Widtsoe, "whether this lineage is of blood or adoption does not matter." (*Evidences and Reconciliations* [Bookcraft, 1960], p. 322.)

There are several reasons why ethnicity and bloodlines are important considerations for Latter-day Saints:

1. They are important in carrying out successful missionary work. In 1909 Elder Charles A. Callis indi-

cated that one day members will teach the restored
gospel to the people of their own countries. (*CR*, April
1909, p. 18.) President George Albert Smith observed
that new converts naturally have anxiety "for those from
whom they descended, the people of their own race."
(*CR*, October 1916, p. 48.) And President Spencer W.
Kimball declared in 1974 that the Church had reached
that state in its history when each nationality and ethnic
group should provide its own missionary force so people
of like ancestry might join together in realizing the full
blessings of the Church.

2. They are important in building convert communities among different races. (See Elder Bruce R. Mc-
Conkie's address to the peoples of Central America and
Mexico at the area conference meetings held August 25-
27, 1972, in the official report of that conference.)

3. They are important in terms of special functions
that have been divinely assigned to different groups of
people in the work of the Lord in the latter days. For
example, the tribe of Ephraim, to which many Latter-
day Saints belong, has been designated to exercise
leadership in administering the affairs of the gospel for
other tribes of Israel in our day. (D&C 133:30-34.)
Judah was designated as the lineage in which the
Messiah would be born, and Levi has been designated to
have special priesthood responsibilities.

However, lineage guarantees no precedence of Israelites over others. It does not guarantee righteousness,
forgiveness of sins, membership in the Church, exaltation in the celestial kingdom, or participation in the
eternal family blessings of Father Abraham. Bloodline
guarantees nothing. The only criterion for receiving
God's blessings is obedience to his laws. Ultimately, the
chosen lineage is the patriarchal chain of righteous
saints; the lineage of faith transcends all distinctions and
barriers of blood. It reconciles God's selection of Israelites as chosen people with God's fatherhood of all
men.

In this manner, all worthy Gentiles become covenant
people, and all unworthy Israelites are cast off. (2 Nephi

30:2.) As Paul said, "they are not all Israel which are of Israel." (Romans 9:6.) John the Baptist, in characteristic bluntness, advised a group of Jews not to rest on their laurels, and to repent of their false belief that their pedigree would save them: "For I say unto you, That God is able of these stones to raise up children unto Abraham." (Luke 3:8.) In like manner, Jesus told another Jewish group, "If ye were Abraham's children, ye would do the works of Abraham. . . . Ye are of your father the devil, and the lusts of your father ye will do." (John 8:39, 44.)

In Mormon doctrine the chosen people are recognized by their faith and righteousness. They meet the requirements for exaltation. When they are cleansed from sin, sealed by the Holy Spirit of Promise, and obtain the power to become gods, they will overcome all things. These are the chosen people, the covenant people; these alone belong to that eternal family which is Israel, the celestial family of God. This eternal family comprises Chinese, Egyptians, Spaniards, Italians, Dutch, Brazilians, Russians, and Samoans. All who magnify their callings in the priesthood become the seed of Abraham and the inheritors of all that God has. (D&C 84:32-38.) Hence, earthly lineage is unimportant in eternity.

Jehovah's concern for Israel has been a concern for all families of the earth. The purpose of Israel's enjoyment of special favor is that all people to the ends of the earth might learn of him through them. Jehovah will finish his saving work with his covenant people by reaching beyond all history to show himself as the God who renews Israel; that is, all worthy men of the earth.

The line of Israel's unity with other peoples is the worship of the true God, who is Jesus Christ. The God of the covenant and the Creator of nations are one. The God of Israel is the God of the whole earth. (3 Nephi 11:14.) Among the children of Israel, in all ages, the spiritual kinship of the convert supersedes any known or supposed genetic foreignness. Conversion makes it possible for any man to belong to the house of Israel and immediately belong to the familial line of the royal seed.

By obedience to the fulness of the gospel, men of all nations become heirs with Christ (who is the natural heir),
can belong to the family of God, and can inherit all that
the Father has.

The fulness of these covenant blessings is conferred
and enjoyed only within the temples of the Church by
those who enter into the order of celestial marriage.
Elder Bruce R. McConkie explains that through marriage in the temple, participants become inheritors of all
the blessings of Abraham; that the only enduring relationships, the only lineage that counts beyond the grave,
are found in that patriarchal chain which begins with
Adam and spreads out until every exalted person is
linked in; and that since there is no special race or family
through which all generations will attain exaltation, the
great patriarchal chain is a lineage of the faithful and
the righteous. (*Mormon Doctrine* [Bookcraft, 1966], pp. 13-
15.) No other lineage will survive.

Thus we see that Israel is not limited to a particular
people or place. Latter-day Israel is not a community of
blood; it is a community of faith. Israel refers to those of
all nations, kindreds, tongues, and peoples who wholeheartedly respond to the will of God.

Old Testament writings generally speak of God as a
father to Israel (Jeremiah 31:9) or the Lord God of Israel
(1 Chronicles 29:10), with little mention of God's fatherhood of all men. New Testament and restoration scriptures, however, explicitly state that all people are
literally children of God. And it is within the framework
of this perception of God as a universal Father that
Latter-day Saints can best appreciate their relationship
to other human beings and God's concern for them.

It is fundamental in Mormon theology that the
entire human race is a family descended from a single
Heavenly Father. All men have not only a physical pedigree leading back to Adam and Eve, the first parents,
but also a spiritual heritage leading back to God. The
physical bodies of mankind were born of earthly parents,
who are all lineal descendants of the same primeval
couple. The spirits of all men were literally born of the

same God before the earth was physically organized. Thus, all persons are literally brothers and sisters in the family of God, and all have the ability, through obedience, to become children of God in a celestial sense. (Romans 8:14, 16-17.)

The Church's obligation to teach and inspire unity and brotherhood among all persons of the world has been given new emphasis in recent months with the announcement on June 9, 1978, that "the long-promised day has come when every faithful, worthy man in the Church may receive the holy priesthood, with power to exercise its divine authority, and enjoy with his loved ones every blessing that flows therefrom, including the blessings of the temple. Accordingly, all worthy male members of the Church may be ordained to the priesthood without regard for race or color. . . . We declare with soberness that the Lord has now made known his will for the blessing of all his children throughout the earth who will hearken to the voice of his authorized servants, and prepare themselves to receive every blessing of the gospel." (*Ensign,* July 1978, p. 75.) At a general conference session on September 30, 1978, this revelation was unanimously accepted by the membership of the Church.

In the gospel view, no man is alien. None are to be denied, and there is no underlying rationale for smugness, arrogance, or pride. Rather, implicit in the gospel is a universal message of life that strikes squarely against all restrictive or stifling traditions based on race, language, place of origin, economic or political standing, educational rank, or cultural background. Led by the apostle Paul, followers of Christ in New Testament times felt compelled to transcend such limiting boundaries. The bitter dispute and painful break are described in detail by Paul and Luke. (Galatians 2 and Acts 15.) Only after receiving a startling vision in which he was instructed that even wild and four-footed beasts are acceptable when God pronounces them clean was the apostle Peter persuaded that Cornelius and the gentiles—and indeed, all men who are willing to obey the gospel—are entitled to fellowship within the Church. In becoming an apostle to the gentiles, Paul was acting upon faith and conviction that no human barriers, natural or fabricated, could exclude any man from the unbounded love of the Lord Jesus Christ. Likewise, Book of Mormon prophets believed that "the Lord esteemeth all flesh as one" (1 Nephi 17:35), and that "all men are privileged the one like unto the other, and none are forbidden," because "he denieth none that come unto him, black and white, bond and free, male and female; and he remembereth the heathen; and all are alike unto God, both Jew and Gentile." (2 Nephi 26:28, 33.) The Prophet Joseph Smith also emphasized that God is not a partial Father; he loves all children alike:

> While one portion of the human race is judging and condemning the other without mercy, the Great Parent of the universe looks upon the whole of the human family with a fatherly care and a parental regard. He views them as His offspring, and without any of those contracted feelings that influence the children of men, causes "His sun to rise on the evil and on the good, sendeth rain on the just and on the unjust." . . . He is a wise Lawgiver, and will judge all men, not according to the narrow, contracted notions of men, but, "according to the deeds done in the body whether they be good or evil," or whether these deeds were done in England, America, Spain, Turkey, or India. (*HC* 4:595-96.)

Jesus set a worthy example of brotherhood when he frequently referred to his disciples as his beloved friends and close associates. He humbly washed his disciples' feet. He suffered little children to come unto him. In his parables of the Good Samaritan and the Lost Sheep, he stressed the innate goodness of every child of God. He taught that for saints the circle of concern includes all men; that our brethren include even those who may be the most unlikely and the most despised. In all his revelations the Lord has commanded his saints to lift one another up, to edify and exalt the children of men. And in this, the law of brotherly love is of first importance. Faultfinding and gossip about the weaknesses of others are condemned as slander because they break down the bonds of brotherhood. Thus, God has admonished that in order to practice virtue and holiness, every man must esteem his brother as himself.

Focusing on this broad human problem of building brotherhood among men, President Spencer W. Kimball, in 1954 while he was a member of the Council of the Twelve, declared that a lack of brotherly love vitally affects the capacity of the Church to fellowship new converts. Sounding a special call for tolerance and understanding of minorities within the Church, he said that Latter-day Saints cannot afford to be complacent with their own shortcomings as a people in inculcating a spirit of genuine brotherhood within the Church, and that all must be vigilant in seeking to eradicate prejudice and hypocrisy.

The worldwide church seeks to assimilate peoples of wide-ranging ethnic and cultural backgrounds. And because of this, the traditional ethnic majority must avoid running the risk of looking upon differences among members as an offense, and upon ethnic minorities as of lesser importance in the kingdom than themselves. President Kimball, in his conference address in April 1954, dealt with the spiritual commitment and the moral ability of the collective church—and in part with whether or not the mainstream membership is fully prepared to accept Orientals, American Indians, Mexicans, and many other racial and cultural minorities who may yet join its ranks.

Implicit here is both a caution and a challenge for all Latter-day Saints—new converts, so-called minority groups, as well as the traditional membership—to shun at all costs false pride, smugness, and ethnocentricity, because these invariably induce and reinforce social divisions, emotional and psychological barriers, and narrow status groups among the members.

The message is simple and clear. The elect of the earth are all those who fully emulate the God of Abraham, who is Jesus Christ. Jesus set a worthy example of love and concern in all his relations with others in his day. True disciples of Christ do not demean, disparage, or condemn. They do not foster bigotry or contention based on differences in race and culture. They reach out with brotherly and familial feelings, and beyond that, as Joseph Smith once observed, "a man filled with the love of God, is not content with blessing his family alone, but ranges through the whole world, anxious to bless the whole human race." (*HC* 4:227.)

Since all Latter-day Saints are of the same spiritual descent, holding the same beliefs, having the same eternal aims, and possessing the same power, they are expected to form a mighty brotherhood, and, according to faithfulness in following the principles of the gospel, in time become the most powerful and privileged people on earth.

4

GATHERINGS
TO ZION

The global expansion of the Church in recent decades has brought changes to the earlier conceptions of Zion as a limited geographical entity. Zion is no longer bound by territory, culture, or nationality. Though the United States has served as a "host" nation in the process of its development, from its inception Joseph Smith emphasized that the Church "is above the kingdoms of this world," that it is not a political entity bound to any one nation, and that it insists upon no claim to political power or secular sway. (*HC* 5:536.) The Church bears the name of the Lord, and the only other designation in the Church's name is dispensational and pertains to time, not to territory.

The building of Zion has been of compelling interest among Latter-day Saints,[1] and among the children of Is-

---

[1]Joseph Smith once wrote: "The building up of Zion is a cause that has interested the people of God in every age; it is a theme upon which prophets, priests and kings have dwelt with particular delight; they have looked forward with joyful anticipation to the day in which we live; and fired with heavenly and joyful anticipations they have sung and written and prophesied of our day; but they died without the sight; we are a favored people that God has made choice of to bring about the Latter-day glory; it is left for us to see, participate in and help to roll forward the Latter-day glory, 'the dispensation of the fulness of times, when God will gather all things that are upon the earth, even in one.' " (*HC* 4:609-10.)

rael since ancient times. It is a concept that has been applied in a great variety of ways, referring at times to
particular geographical locations. Biblical prophets
wrote of Jerusalem as the city of Zion. (2 Samuel 5:7; 1
Kings 8:1.) The Pearl of Great Price speaks of the city of
Enoch as the Zion of the Lord. (Moses 7:18.) In the Doctrine and Covenants, the city of the New Jerusalem in
Jackson County, Missouri, is also called the city of Zion
(D&C 57:1-2), where Christ will administer the affairs of
his people in the coming millennium. Salt Lake City is
often referred to as Zion, since it is the headquarters of
the Church.

In 1844, Joseph Smith referred to the whole of North
and South America as the land of Zion (*HC* 6:318-19),
leading many to believe that it was limited to those two
continents. But in an extraordinary statement in 1861,
Brigham Young stressed the need of a more encompass-
ing view, that Zion would one day become truly worldwide: "Zion will extend eventually over all of this earth
of ours. There will be no nook or corner upon the earth
but that will one day be in Zion, a part of the work of
God. It will all be thus." (*JD* 9:138.)

This conception of a worldwide Zion might appear
surprising to those who have been accustomed to a more
limited view. Far more important than location, though,
is the spirit of Zion, the spiritual achievement of the
people of God. Brigham Young indicated this when he
stated that the Saints should gather to Utah to establish
Zion without expecting to find it in all its glory: "We
can make Zion, or we can make Babylon, just as we
please. We can make just what we please out of this
place. The people can make Zion: they can make a
heaven within themselves, with the resolution that I will
carry myself full of the Spirit of Zion wherever I go; . . .
and do you not see that such a course will make Zion?"
(*JD* 5:4.)

Latter-day scriptures identify Zion as the kingdom of
God (D&C 105:32), and the righteous saints as the
people of the kingdom. In the time of Enoch, "the Lord
called his people Zion, because they were of one heart

and one mind, and dwelt in righteousness; and there was no poor among them."(Moses 7:18.) Zion is also viewed as a qualitative condition, implying personal sanctification through the submission of one's will to God. (D&C 82:19.) Zion communities are to be brought forth in the modern world upon the same principle as Enoch's Zion—by seeking the interest of one's neighbors and keeping one's eyes single to the glory of God.

Elder Matthew Cowley instructed Latter-day Saints throughout the world that "in your homes where the priesthood of God exists, there is Zion. And to you whose lives are committed to righteousness, I say to you, you are Zion." (CR, April 1952, p. 102.) Brigham Young had earlier concluded: "As to the spirit of Zion, it is in the hearts of the saints, of those who love and serve the Lord with all their might, mind, and strength. . . . and unless the people live before the Lord in obedience of his commandments, they cannot have Zion within them, if they expect to live in it, to enjoy it, and increase in it. If they do not do this, they are as much destitute of Zion here as they are in other places." (JD 2:253.) And Joseph Smith received a revelation from God that stated: "Let Zion rejoice, for this is Zion—the pure in heart." (D&C 97:21.)

Members of The Church of Jesus Christ of Latter-day Saints teach and believe that Moses, the prophet and lawgiver of ancient Israel, appeared in vision to Joseph Smith and Oliver Cowdery on April 3, 1836. He committed to them "the keys of the gathering of Israel from the four parts of the earth." (D&C 110:11.) Other revelations were unequivocal in their insistence that this latter-day gathering would lead to the establishment of Zion, and that it should be instituted without delay. (D&C 63:24; 133:4, 9.) The first gatherings started in Ohio and Missouri, then Illinois, reaching their culmination at the end of the trail in valleys bordering the Wasatch Mountains in what is now Utah, where the Saints established a kingdom far removed from the world at large. By 1855, any Saint who failed to gather not only to the United States but also to Utah was con-

sidered to be in violation of God's explicit commands.
(*JD* 2:252.) All faithful converts were expected to emigrate to Utah, where the purity of Zion could be
enjoyed. To remain at Jackson County, Missouri, or
Nauvoo, Illinois, was no longer sufficient. Willingness to
gather to the Rocky Mountains was a mark of faithfulness and obedience.

In the early days, Church membership consisted almost entirely of North Americans, Englishmen, Scandi-
navians, Germans, and other Western peoples who immigrated to Utah to enjoy the fellowship of the Saints.
The spirit of physical gathering was strong among the
people. Since most of the converts were of European
origins, there was a genetic and special interest in identi-
fying peoples of Caucasian descent with the house of Israel. Israel was often regarded as an exclusive and
limited community of blood.

Once situated in the settlements of Utah,
mainstream modern Israel became a unified and homo-
geneous people bound together by a common heritage, a
common ancestry, common historical experience (the
persecutions, the trek west, the hardships of coloniza-
tion), a common language (only English was spoken in
the general conferences of the Church), and a common
European religious background. Members derived primarily from Protestant and Catholic mission fields, who
perceived the restored gospel from the vantage point of
Christian traditions, values, and institutions associated
with such developments as the European Renaissance,
the Reformation, and the Industrial Revolution. But the
Church was founded and nurtured in American soil.
Scriptural injunctions attesting to a divinity in the underlying principles of the American form of government,
including emphasis upon the land of America as a land
of promise, choice above all other lands, gave strength
within the Church to a decidedly American nationalism.

By the end of the nineteenth century Americanism,
Americanization, and Mormonism became intrinsically
synonymous in the lives of the pioneer Saints. The celebration of the 4th of July, which involved rededication

to the United States, its flag, its institutions, and its history, was as much a symbolic act of unity as was the 24th of July celebration of the arrival of the pioneers in the Salt Lake Valley. Historically speaking, the Church came to be regarded as a cultural and geographic entity, distinctly American in character and style, with Utah as its sacred centerplace. Euphoric and nostalgic feelings for Utah as "the Zion of the Lord," the hearth and homeland of all faithful Saints, were frequently expressed in sermons, poems, and songs throughout the Church, but never more effectively than in these words from the hand of Charles W. Penrose, an English convert who immigrated to America and eventually became a member of the First Presidency:

> O Zion!
> Dear Zion!
> Land of the free,
> Now my own mountain home,
> Unto thee I have come,
> All my fond hopes are centered in thee.
> —*Hymns*, no. 145

A 1972 survey suggests that even then, most Mormons considered Utah as a holy place, exceeded in sacredness only by the future New Jerusalem in Jackson County, Missouri.[2] This attitude and the Mormon belief that a truly valiant Saint would reside only in the Great Basin of the American West were no doubt historically rooted in concern for the welfare of Zion.

The gathering to Zion resulted in a vibrant, unified church in western America. But it was never intended that the Great Basin kingdom would be the final resting place of the Church. The establishment of Zion in America through the gathering of modern Israel was not invariably regarded as an ultimate end in itself. Rather, some Church leaders from very early times viewed this as an essential interim development leading to an ultimate destiny of building up Zion throughout the world.

---

[2]Roger L. Henrie, "The Perception of Sacred Space: The Case of Utah and Other Sacred Places in Mormonism," unpublished master's thesis, Brigham Young University, 1972.

The Saints gathered to Ohio, Missouri, and Illinois to form a central unit of strength for the Church. They were only partially successful there. In time they were driven from their lands. They then fled to the Rocky Mountains to find a place of refuge that America might become a base of operations, a centerplace of Zion. The ultimate objective of the physical gathering to Utah was to build up what Daniel H. Wells in 1860 called "a nucleus of power" (JD 8:93), for carrying out a much larger enterprise. Orson F. Whitney cautioned the Saints in 1910 that this could not be accomplished "until we have sufficient numbers and strength." (CR, April 1910, p. 86.) As the Church grew, the center gained that strength, and the guidance on a physical gathering began to shift. As early as 1898, instructions from the First Presidency began to stress a spiritual gathering of the Saints in multiple Zion communities throughout the world. In that year, members outside the United States were first given counsel to stay in their native lands:

> Do not send the saints here from abroad, but rather keep them in the branches until they get grounded in the faith. . . . now it is not the voice of the Spirit that the saints should gather from the nations of the earth as they have been doing. . . . In this way, we may raise up strong branches, that will assist the Elders in the various fields of labor. (George Q. Cannon, CR, April 1898, p. 8.)

> By having the Saints remain in the places where they dwell they gain experience and strength. Besides this, they are able to help the Elders, and the Elders do not find it so difficult to preach the gospel, because they have the support and assistance of those who are members of the Church and who live in organized branches of the Church. (George Q. Cannon, CR, October 1898, p. 8.)

The Saints were counseled to become grounded in the faith, and then to come to Utah only to receive temple ordinances; settling in Utah was also sometimes discouraged because of the lack of employment for new settlers.

Although the First Presidency continued its efforts to discourage converts from leaving their native lands and gathering to Utah, it was not until after World War II that a really marked change could be observed. With the end of World War II, the Church entered a dramatic new era of growth and development on a global scale. It was the beginning of a self-conscious and energetic effort to become a truly universal organization. President David O. McKay was uniquely prepared by experience, education, personality, and prophetic office to direct the work. He had toured the world as a member of the Twelve in 1921, had visited the countries of Asia, and had dedicated China for the preaching of the gospel. By 1963 at least half of all living Latter-day Saints had known no other president of the Church, not only because of his long tenure, but also because of the great growth and expansion as new converts formed a larger proportion of the membership.

President McKay's great emphasis on worldwide missionary work—"every member a missionary"—was matched by his own worldwide ministrations. In 1951, he made the first of several trips to Europe. In 1954, he made a 32,000-mile trip to South Africa and South America. The following year he traveled 45,000 miles to visit missions in the South Pacific. He became the best known and most widely traveled Mormon president in history. The mark of his administration was a conscious effort to give dignity and strength to the Church in areas outside the United States.

Under David O. McKay's presidency basic features of Zion were first established in foreign fields: stakes were organized in the South Pacific and in Europe; temples were erected in New Zealand, Switzerland, and England; missions were organized among peoples, cultures, and nations previously beyond the purview of the mainstream church. The physical gathering was now suspended, and a new emphasis on spiritual gathering continued unabated.

The end of the physical gathering meant the beginning of a new buoyancy for the Church in many parts of the world, particularly in Europe, which had traditionally been drained of leadership, stability, and growth. The remarks of Matthew Cowley in a general conference address in April 1952 reaffirmed these new directions in Church development. Speaking to "the people of Great Britain, in the Scandinavian countries, in Holland, in Germany, in Czechoslovakia, France, Switzerland, Austria, Palestine, South Africa, the South American nations, those who dwell within the great Polynesian triangle in the Pacific, and to those fine people few in number, in the far-off Orient," he said, "I would like to say to you that I know that in your hearts this day there is a longing to be here at the hub of this great Church, a longing which you cannot realize. . . . You are needed where you are." (*CR*, April 1952, p. 102.)

At the first Mexico and Central America area conference held at Mexico City in August 1972, Elder Bruce R. McConkie delivered a discourse of historic significance, dealing with the gathering of Israel in the contemporary Church. In what must be regarded as a doctrinal benchmark, Elder McConkie spoke of many lands of promise and inheritance, of many gatherings worldwide.

This gathering has commenced and shall continue until the righteous are assembled into the congregations of the Saints in all the nations of the earth. "I will gather the remnant of my flock out of all countries whither I have driven them," the Lord says, "and will bring them to their folds; and they shall be fruitful and increase."

Nephi teaches this truth in these words: "The Lord God will proceed to make bare his arm in the eyes of all the nations in bringing about *his covenants* and *his gospel* unto those who are of the house of Israel. Wherefore, he will bring them again out of captivity, and they shall be gathered together to the *lands of their inheritance;* and they shall be brought out of obscurity and out of darkness; and *they shall know that the Lord is their Savior and their Redeemer, and the Mighty One of Israel.*"

In other words, the gathering to Zion during this "culminating era" of Church history consists of joining in fellowship in congregations of Saints throughout the world. The quality of Zion may be one but its locations are many. And, according to Elder McConkie, all nationalities and peoples are entitled to regard their own countries as special gathering places, as lands of the Lord:

The place of gathering for the Mexican Saints is in Mexico; the place of gathering for the Guatemalan Saints is in Guatemala; the place of gathering for the Brazilian, Brazil; and so it goes throughout the length and breadth of the whole earth. Japan is for the Japanese; Korea is for the Koreans; Australia is for the Australians; every nation is the gathering place for its own people.

That Zion should now be viewed in a new way—as a single spiritual and moral community that expresses itself in a challenging variety of geographical and cultural patterns—was also emphasized by President Harold B. Lee during the April 1973 general conference. He first quoted the Lord concerning the kingdom of God: "For Zion must increase in beauty, and in holiness; her borders must be enlarged; her stakes must be strengthened; yea, verily I say unto you Zion must arise and put on her beautiful garments." (D&C 82:14.) Then, speaking of the Church, he explained:

Her boundaries are being enlarged, her stakes are being strengthened. In the early years of the Church specific places to which the Saints were to be gathered together were given and the Lord directed that these places should not be changed. . . . No longer might this church be thought of as the "Utah church," or as an "American church," but the membership of the Church is now distributed over the earth in 78 countries, teaching the gospel in 17 different languages at the present time. This greatly expanded Church population is today our most challenging problem. . . . (*Ensign*, July 1973, p. 4.)

New efforts to build up Zion through multiple gatherings has required serious readjustments and changes. This is suggested in instructions of the First Presidency given in August 1973 regarding the Polynesian "colony" at Laie, Hawaii:

It was felt [in earlier times] that the Saints in those areas needed to have a gathering place in order to maintain their identity and not become lost among the nations of man and overcome by the world.

With the stakes now being established in New Zealand, Samoa, Tonga, and Tahiti, and with the advent of temples being built in overseas areas of the Church, *the need for the gathering as spoken of by President Joseph F. Smith and others has been satisfied, and to a large measure we are past that station in our history. As people join the Church in the different countries, they are encouraged to join together in their own lands and meet and learn and teach the gospel in their own tongue,* and thereby build and organize branches and stakes where they meet together often and are entitled to all the blessings promised to the faithful Saints. By doing this they will be building the Church and kingdom of God here upon the earth. As the cords are lengthened and the stakes are strengthened throughout the world, the work of the Lord will go forward. (Letter of the First Presidency to Faaesea P. Mailo, dated August 21, 1973. Italics added.)

Later that same year, President Lee referred to the remarkable contribution of the British and other European Saints who had earlier joined the Church and immigrated to America. (*Ensign*, August 1973, pp. 3-4.) He observed that the early Saints were commanded to gather to the American Zion so they might receive spiritual blessings found only within the temples of God, but that a new worldwide spirit had taken over in the Church, particularly since World War II, because temples were being erected in all lands where members reside in numbers. He called on Mormons everywhere to remain steadfast in their native countries and to find happiness in helping to build up Zion in their respective lands.

In this book are found the stories of several families who sought to heed the direction of the prophets with regard to the spirit of gathering. Some emigrated to America; some stayed in their own lands to build and strengthen the Church there. Several came to Utah, in part to enjoy the blessings of the temple, and some later returned to their homes to continue to serve.

5

EDUCATING
THE SAINTS

From the Isle of Wight to the outback of Australia; from the Yucatan Peninsula to Korea and Japan; from the highlands of Peru to the coast of South Africa— wherever the Saints and the missionary program can be found, the Church is reaching out to provide educational opportunities to youth, to college students, and to persons of all ages.*

In a revelation given through the Prophet Joseph Smith in March 1836, the Lord declared: "And as all have not faith, seek ye diligently and teach one another words of wisdom; yea, seek ye out of the best books words of wisdom, seek learning even by study and also by faith." (D&C 109:7.) One of the greatest challenges of the Church as it moves into an era of worldwide

---

*The flagship of the Church's educational system is Brigham Young University, the largest privately owned university in the United States, with 25,000 students from all states of the U.S. and many foreign countries. No other single educational operation in the Church does as much to prepare Latter-day Saint youth in religious education and professional training. BYU includes a campus at Laie, Hawaii; in addition, the church operates Ricks College in Rexburg, Idaho, and other schools in Mexico and the islands of the Pacific. This chapter, however, concerns itself primarily with religious education for high school and selected college-level students in seminaries and institutes of religion in far-flung areas of the world.

growth is to strengthen the members and teach the principles of the gospel. The Lord has directed that the Saints are to carry the gospel to every nation, kindred, tongue, and people; and in order to achieve this goal, it is necessary that every member and prospective member be able to read the scriptures and other Church manuals and books and understand them through an organized program of learning.

Religious education in the Church began on a spring morning in 1820 when fourteen-year-old Joseph Smith, Jr., entered the woods near Palmyra, New York, and knelt in prayer. There he prayed fervently for religious knowledge; he wanted to know which of all the churches would teach him the truth. In response to that prayer two glorious personages appeared to him: God the Father and his Son, Jesus Christ. This visitation set in motion a sequence of communications between heaven and earth designed to lead men back into the presence of God.

The heavenly instructions were simple, powerful, and demanding. They required commitment, dedication, and sacrifice. Sacred writings, spiritual confirmations, and priesthood powers were made available to the newly called prophet and his followers, but they had to learn and grow in the Lord's way: precept upon precept, line upon line, here a little and there a little. It soon became evident that the plan of salvation for mankind was a program of education in its broadest sense: learning who we are, where we came from, why we are here, and what we must do to fulfill our divine nature as sons and daughters of God.

The need for using printed materials to accelerate the learning process in the Church has been obvious from the beginning. There is much the members need to learn, and literacy—man's unique power to read and write—has magnified the impact of verbal testimony. Thus the Church has broadened the scope of its educational programs, which in the Prophet Joseph Smith's day were concentrated on printing the Book of Mormon and other Church literature as well as on conducting a school for priesthood leaders. As the Church became more established in the Rocky Mountains, and the administration more centralized in the church headquarters, religion classes and Church academies or schools for youth were organized under a general board of education. These evolved into what are known today as seminaries and institutes of religion.

President David O. McKay once observed that "the spirituality of a ward will be commensurate with the activity of the youth in that ward." This has been one of the guiding principles underlying the educational programs. And by extension, the strength and spirituality of the entire church are largely commensurate with the activity of its youth. In this, the role of religious education greatly influences the vitality of the expanding church.

In 1975 the Department of Seminaries and Institutes of Religion formulated and published its overall goals and objectives. These included "three pillars of emphasis":

First, . . . helping young people recognize and mature in their eternal relationship with God, with fellowmen and with self. . . .

Second, . . . to employ energetic men of faith, character, and integrity—competent men who are young in feeling, who love youth, who command their respect and admiration, and who are capable of exercising an influence for good over them; individuals who are true friends of education. . . .

Third, . . . developing an instructional environment that encourages a companionship between the youth and the restored gospel of Christ.

Religious education for youth is concentrated in four major programs, three for youths in junior high schools and high schools and one for those who are attending colleges. They are:

1. *Home-study seminary*. This program is applicable where there are insufficient numbers of Mormon youths to hold either early-morning or released-time seminary, and is widely used in parts of the southern and eastern states of the United States, Canada, Australia, New Zealand, the United Kingdom, South America, South

Africa, Asia, and many European countries. In this program the young people generally spend about thirty minutes daily reading the assigned course of study (one of the standard works of scripture) with a supplemental workbook; about one hour a week with other students from their ward or branch and with a teacher, to discuss the lesson assignments; and one Saturday a month with youths of the region, for discussion, instruction, and social activities.

2. *Early-morning seminary.* Throughout the United States, Canada, and in various parts of Australia, New Zealand, the United Kingdom, and other places, tens of thousands of Latter-day Saint youths meet before school for an hour to take the current seminary course of study, under the direction of a competent seminary instructor. These classes are usually held in a ward or branch chapel in the early morning hours, after which the youths go to their regular junior high or high school classes. Once a year or oftener they get together with other seminary groups in the area for a youth convocation or other planned activities.

3. *Released-time seminary.* In some parts of the United States, primarily in the Rocky Mountain area, school boards have granted permission for Latter-day Saint youths as well as nonmembers to attend seminary classes during the regular school day under released time. These classes are generally taught in seminary buildings adjacent to the school campuses.

4. *Institute of religion.* Latter-day Saint students and nonmembers may enroll in classes taught at institutes of religion adjacent to many colleges, universities, and vocational or trade schools throughout the United States and in many other countries. The courses of study range from marriage preparation to missionary preparation; science and religion to religions of the world; as well as in-depth study of the scriptures.

President Spencer W. Kimball voiced the objectives of the seminary and institute programs in an address to Regional Representatives of the Twelve in 1975 when he said:

The goal of every Latter-day Saint is eternal life or exaltation. This can best be achieved by following the straight and narrow path which leads to this goal; namely, participation in the seminary and institute program, a mission, and an eternal marriage. In seminaries and institutes youth are encouraged to fulfill and are assisted in training for a mission. Almost all of those who do fulfill an honorable mission marry in the temple. Those who keep the vows made in the temple will inherit eternal life.

Weekday religious training is in a position to do as much as any instructional program in the Church to assist the home in directly helping youth achieve eternal life. I strongly advise all youth to continue on this path by participating in the seminary and institute program.

The Saints throughout the world are heeding the words of President Kimball and the other Brethren. Enrollment in seminary and institute classes has shown a marked increase in recent years, more missionaries than ever before are being called, and there has been an increase in the number of young couples who are setting their goals for temple marriage.

In 1975 an article in the *Ensign* reported that "five years ago very few temple marriages were performed for young New Zealand couples, and calls for missionary service were infrequent. This year, a single institute class reported fourteen temple marriages, and one stake called as many missionaries as were called in all of New Zealand in past years—and nearly all of these missionaries are seminary graduates." (Lane Johnson, "When Schools Are Few," *Ensign*, December 1975, p. 20.)

The *Church News* on October 23, 1976, reported that "since the seminary and institute program began in Venezuela in 1973, enrollment has grown from 110 to 850 students between the ages of 13 and 17 for seminary and 18 and 28 for institute. Zulay Pacheco of the Caracas 3rd Branch, Venezuela Caracas Mission, a lady missionary in her country, said, 'The simple ways in which I learned the truths of the gospel in my studies in seminary have helped in my mission to teach my investigators.' " Church leaders in that country noted that testimony meetings in each branch of the mission nearly always included testimonies of young people who shared their gratitude for their seminary course or teacher.

In Buenos Aires, Argentina, several young people expressed their feelings about the institute program, which was first introduced in that city in 1975:

Patricio Hortal found that "college study is very important for our progression. If a Latter-day Saint has a strong testimony of the gospel, when he enters college and acquires new and more profound knowledge, his testimony will grow even more." He added, "The institute has been a great help to me. I have gained knowledge and great insight. It is an ensign to youth and influences us to make correct decisions about our college education."

Martha Lorca said, "I think that the institute is a large source of help to our testimonies. I feel truly blessed because of the knowledge given in its classrooms. It has helped me decide to be useful in Zion. I have come to a better understanding as to why our Father in Heaven gives us commandments. The guidance and help received from the teachers has been very important to me." She continued, "The institute helps us resolve many conflicts in our studies. It has been put here to serve the youth and help us now and will do it more in the future."

Estela Maria Vlera said, "During the classes I feel happy for the opportunity the Lord has given me to progress. I have learned better ways to assimilate the truth and put it into practice. It has helped me better serve my fellowman and therefore be a better daughter to our Father in Heaven." (*Church News*, July 31, 1976.)

One area in which the Church's religious education program has had an especially striking impact is in the teaching of Indian youths. The Indian seminary program serves over forty tribes in twenty states and five Canadian provinces, and reaches some 12,500 Indian students. The curriculum is especially adapted for American Indians, and in some areas is providing religious instruction for children as young as kindergarten age.

In a report on the Indian seminary program in December 1975, it was reported that "seminary is leaving a marked impression on the lives of many students, among them Lorenzo Curley, a Navajo boy introduced to the gospel through seminary one year ago during his first year of high school. Lorenzo was chosen to represent his seminary with a fellow student, a recent convert, at a seminary 'scripture chase' event in St. Johns, Arizona. Though the two Indian boys lacked the three other members necessary to form a scripture chase team, they competed with the Anglo teams, each made up of five lifelong members of the Church known for their past achievements in seminary work. Despite odds that seemed so great, Lorenzo and his partner won the competition 50 to 0." (Chris L. Jones, "Seminary for Six-Year-Olds," *Ensign*, December 1975, p. 22.)

One of the largest Church educational programs in the world is in Korea, where over 1,400 students are attending institutes of religion and more than 1,000 students are enrolled in seminary. Korea was also the first country outside the United States and Canada to have a building built especially for institute classes.

At the first open house held in Seoul to explain the institute program a few years ago, plans were made to accommodate from fifty to one hundred guests; but over three hundred crowded into the meeting room, and because of lack of adequate space, many more were turned away. Within two and a half years enrollment exceeded eight hundred.

Ho Nam Rhee, coordinator for seminaries and institutes in Korea, reported in a *Church News* interview on April 16, 1977, that the Koreans' hunger for knowledge and education "is one of the reasons why the institute program is so successful in Korea. . . . I'm so grateful for the institute program. The gospel is really changing the lives of young people. They are now overcoming old superstitions and walking in the Mormon pattern of life. A new lifestyle is being created. If we want to gain good husbands, good wives and loving parents, we must have this new lifestyle, while still maintaining our Korean heritage."

Another area in which the program is gaining momentum is in the British Isles, where seminary and institute enrollment increased from 164 in 1968 to 4,700 by mid-1977. Seminary classes in the British Isles are all home-study classes, but efforts are being made to establish early-morning groups in the near future. "Seminary classes are a wonderful missionary tool," reports David Cook, coordinator for seminaries and institutes in the British Isles. "There are about 150 young people in the classes who would like to be members but don't have their parents' permission to join the Church. We even have some four-year seminary graduates who are nonmembers." (*Church News*, April 16, 1977.)

Youth enrollment in the Church-sponsored religion classes exerts a strong influence on the regular church activity of both young and old. Robert B. Arnold, who served as president of the Guatemala-El Salvador Mission, reported that attendance in a branch in El Salvador had dwindled to approximately eight persons a week. Then twenty-one young people in the branch enrolled in seminary. Three months later the average attendance had increased to over fifty, and by the end of the year the branch was building a new chapel. Both the mission president and the branch members were convinced that the seminary program had "resurrected" the branch.

One of the exciting outgrowths of seminary and institute participation has been the development of "share projects." Recognizing that special needs exist in some areas of the Church, students have been encouraged to join together and pool their resources to share with those who are less fortunate in other parts of the world.

Seminary students in Finland have shared the results of their efforts with seminary students in Samoa, where a former Finnish student was serving as a health missionary. Seminary students in other areas have donated their own recreation monies, sacrificed special treats, and performed special services to earn funds to contribute to a share project. Audiovisual projectors, tape recorders, duplicating machines, and other educational equipment have been provided through these funds. In some instances share funds have been used to provide travel and food so students in poorer areas might have the opportunity to meet together. More than a score of LDS libraries have been established with share funds. In the first three years of the program's operation over a quarter of a million dollars was contributed for distribution on a student-sharing-with-a-student basis.

Educating the Saints doesn't end with the seminary and institute programs, however. The Church has established more than sixty elementary and middle schools, eight secondary schools, one preparatory school, and one normal school in the Pacific Islands and Latin America.

In South America the secular education program was started in Chile with four schools, and the movement soon spread to other countries. The Church has established secular schools in these areas because educational opportunities are not as readily available, and numerous children would have no formal schooling without them. The policy of the Church has been to provide secular education where the state has not supplied it, and to withdraw from secular education whenever and wherever public schools have become adequate.

One of the most successful of these programs is found in Mexico, where many thousands of students are enrolled in schools scattered from Tijuana in the north, through cities and towns large and small all the way south to Tapachula, near the Guatemalan border. More than 80 percent of the students are Latter-day Saints, and they come to the Church schools from every state in Mexico and from Central America. Benemerito de las Americas is the largest of these schools, located on a large ranch near Mexico City.

More than 2,000 students in grades one through twelve are enrolled at Benemerito. They live and study on a campus that now has more than seventy buildings. The students are assigned to groups of sixteen, with each group living in a cottage supervised by a couple serving as parents. These groups function much as a family, with family activities, family home evenings, and family prayer. The children help to prepare meals, perform household duties, and attend church together.

Many of the students at Benemerito are employed on the campus, where they receive experience as secretaries, clerks, maintenance crews, and teachers' aides to help defray their educational expenses. The students receive an excellent education, and those who apply for admission to Mexican universities following graduation from Benemerito generally achieve high scores on their entrance examinations. One of the supervisors of the Church's primary school system declared, "Our schools have an outstanding academic record in Mexico. They are noted for their sound learning environment and for the personal, moral integrity of their teaching staff. What parent would not want to have his children learn not only how to read and write effectively, but also to be honest, to have integrity and character?" (Paul James Toscano, "Church Education in Mexico," *Ensign*, September 1972, pp. 34-39.)

Though the main thrust of the Church's educational programs is aimed at youth and college-age students, the Church is also concerned about the education of adults who have had little opportunity to learn the basic skills of reading, writing, and arithmetic. An innovative tutoring program that is achieving dramatic results was described in an article in the *Ensign* in December 1975:

Illiteracy . . . hampers Church members. They can't read the scriptures or the Church tracts; they can't prepare gospel lessons, study the teachings of the prophets, or benefit from the many Church-produced training programs. Consequently, many otherwise talented people suffer spiritually because they cannot read their own language.

Illiteracy is a problem that all governments put high on their educational priorities; but sometimes adults are neglected when limited resources are allocated to educate the children. The Church, keenly aware that each life is precious *now*, has established schools and encouraged reading programs by local priesthood leaders; but recently, a new solution to the illiteracy problem among adult members of the Church has been inaugurated by the Church Educational System's Division of Continuing Education.

The program is called "Structured Tutoring." It spells out proper teaching methods clearly, simply, and sequentially so that nonprofessionals with little or no teaching experience can tutor their friends and associates in reading, writing, and basic arithmetic. Structured tutoring was orginally developed . . . as a way to teach elementary school children in the United States how to read.

In 1971, Church leaders decided to use this same system to train a small group of Bolivian Saints to read Spanish, using Spanish tutor/student manuals and nonprofessional Bolivian members as tutors.

Since then hundreds of adults have learned to read, and the program is now being experimented with in many places throughout the Lamanite world. The success of the program is reflected by their spiritual and temporal growth. . . .

By the end of 1974, there were 213 students in the Bolivia program with a total of 223 tutors on call. Forty-six out of the 102 non-LDS students and twelve out of twenty non-LDS tutors have been baptized. To date, over 1,000 people have graduated from the program—equivalent to approximately 18 percent of the total Church population in Bolivia. . . .

How does the literacy program add up in dollars and cents? The total cost of teaching one person to read is a mere $12. This figure includes local administrative expenses and the cost of materials and supplies. . . . Literacy now is economically feasible for everyone, a doorway into the future the Church is opening for a multitude of members. . . .

To meet increasing demands, materials are now being developed to teach writing and elementary math, and the entire program is being extended to other parts of South America, Mexico, and Central America. (Paul James Toscano, "Attack on Illiteracy," *Ensign*, December 1975, pp. 16-18.)

Still another way in which the Church is providing help for the education of the Saints is a scholarship fund established by the Church Educational System in 1974. Under this program, worthy members in underdeveloped countries can qualify either for loans or for educational grants. As loans are repaid and as those who receive grants begin to contribute to the scholarship fund at a later date, these resources in turn become available to others who need assistance. In this way, the scholarship fund functions much like the Perpetual Emigration Fund that operated in the early days of the Church: those who received money for passage to America paid money back into the fund when they were able so that others might follow.

Through these varied educational programs, the Church is demonstrating its deep commitment to helping its members develop to the fullest potential by removing barrriers to educational opportunities wherever possible. As expansion takes the Church into other lands, the Educational System is expanding also, developing programs to fit the needs of the members.

6

FOR THE HEALTH OF THE SAINTS

As the Church extends its love, care, and concern among peoples in many far-flung lands, it also accepts the challenge to help those peoples find physical as well as spiritual well-being. In the Book of Mormon the prophet Jacob writes:

"But before ye seek for riches, seek ye for the kingdom of God.

"And after ye have obtained a hope in Christ ye shall obtain riches, if ye seek them; and ye will seek them for the intent to do good—to clothe the naked, and to feed the hungry, and to liberate the captive, and administer relief to the sick and the afflicted." (Jacob 2:18-19.)

Latter-day Saints are a sharing people, a giving people. They are eager to share the truths of the gospel with their brothers and sisters throughout the world. And as they do so, they also go the second mile, following the admonitions of Jacob and other prophets through all dispensations. They share with others the joys that come through feeling good and living in healthy conditions.

One of the most exciting programs of the Church in

recent years as it expands worldwide is the calling of health services missionaries to teach proper nutrition and sanitation habits, care of children, first aid, and home nursing in areas where there is a need for such information and help. Their calling is to teach preventive measures rather than practice medicine or care for patients. They also encourage those whom they meet to make wise use of local health services.

The health missionary program places physicians, nutritionists, dentists, dental hygienists, home economists, health educators, and others in health teaching assignments in various missions. In addition to their assignment to teach good health practices, they also teach investigators the principles of the gospel.

Each of the missionaries called for this special service has been given specific instructions to echo in his ministrations the philosophy of Joseph Smith when a certain lawyer asked about his success in "controlling" the people. The Prophet replied, "I do not govern the people. I teach them correct principles and they govern themselves." (Quoted by Erastus Snow, *JD* 24:159.) In other words, health service missionaries are expected to teach correct principles of healthful living. They are "not actually involved in providing health care or giving 'things' to members of the Church. They are called as teachers, not practitioners." (*Church News*, December 8, 1973, editorial page.)

Dr. James O. Mason, former Church Health Commissioner, said that the missionaries were instructed to emphasize prevention of disease and to help local Church leaders teach the Saints how to maintain good health. "Our experience has shown what numerous studies have proved: that prevention is far more effective in improving the health of the population and is much less expensive in terms of personnel, facilities and funds, than is treatment," he declared. (Paper presented to the General Priesthood Committee, September 1973.)

Edward L. Soper, who served as assistant health commissioner, elaborated on these instructions:

If you think about the instructions given to us in the 89th section of the Doctrine and Covenants, commonly called the Word of Wisdom, you will see that compliance with these instructions helps us to maintain good health and helps to prevent, rather than to cure disease. The Word of Wisdom does not, for example, tell us how to cure cancer of the lung. On the other hand, it tells us clearly how to prevent cancer of the lung; that is, through the avoidance of the use of tobacco. So you see, its emphasis on prevention provides a good health pattern for members of the Church to follow. (Address on KBYU, Provo, Utah, April 2, 1972.)

Each health services missionary works within the priesthood organization. Each is responsible to a mission president. Each is assigned a missionary companion. And each works within the local ecclesiastical organizations, training Relief Society presidencies, branch presidencies, quorum leaders, and others.

Marilyn Lyons, a registered nurse who was serving as a proselyting missionary in the Oklahoma Mission, became the first health missionary when she was transferred to the Tonga Mission in July 1971. She later reported, "The health mission has been the best of two missions, because I got to proselyte and was able to get into people's homes using health information." (*Church News*, January 6, 1973.) Sister Lyons, who has a master's degree in nursing education, also worked closely with the Liahona High School, the Church's high school in Tonga, to set up a nurses' aide teaching program at the school while on her mission.

Mary Ellen Edmunds, who labored in the Philippines, wrote in the *New Era:*

When I first received a call to serve as a health missionary, I knew very little about the program. I had a vision of myself heading into the deep, dark jungle, mounted on a carabao, laden down with an eighteen-month supply of Band-Aids, aspirin, multi-colored fly swatters, rubbing alcohol, shoelaces, insect repellent, obsolete snakebite kits, bouillon cubes, and various first-aid manuals collected from MIA and physical education classes.

This dream has been shattered in the months I've been serving in the Philippines as a health missionary, but the vision that has taken its place is so beautiful, I don't miss the carabao at all! . . .

Contrary to what many of us believed when we first heard of the program, we are not sent out to cure all the diseases on the face of the earth. We are not even called to treat the illnesses of the members of the Church but rather to teach them the principles of good health that will help them prevent disease. What a beautiful program!

... We have the advantage of a perfect organization already established and the direction of the priesthood. What a perfect way to reach the family and the individual--through the Church program, which is already functioning all over the world! We will work with and train leaders who will then share with the members. Under the direction of the district and branch leaders and our mission president, we will help to gather resource material, determine health problems in specific areas, and formulate lessons, programs, and activities that can be adapted to various teaching situations. Because of the way our program will work, and the emphasis on health care rather than sick care, we can establish something that will endure long after we've gone home. (*New Era*, June 1973, p. 52.)

The importance of the work of the health missionaries was pointed out in a talk by Dr. Mason in the priesthood session of general conference in October 1971, shortly after the program was announced. He reported:

How often we take for granted those things that we enjoy and participate in almost every day--the hospitals, the physicians, the dentists, the nurses, and other professional people who render services.

Read with me a letter that came from the Philippine Islands, from a dear sister who pleaded, "Can our family share with you who live in the United States the blessings of good health, the Primary Children's Hospital, and other facilities where you go to keep your children healthy and strong?" She told how it was necessary to go great distances to find doctors and a hospital.

Go with me to hear a branch president in an Indian village in Guatemala. Hear as he explains how four of his nine children died before they reached the age of five because of improper nutrition and poor sanitation, which resulted in dysentery, pneumonia, and other illnesses.

Walk with me into the home of an Indian family living on the high plains of Bolivia. The husband serves as the branch Sunday School superintendent and his wife is the Primary president. See their six-week-old infant daughter dying of starvation because their meager income of eight dollars a month makes them unable to provide food for their baby when the mother becomes sick and is unable to nurse.

Travel with me to a large government hospital, newly built in Tonga and equipped to provide needed services to members and

nonmembers alike. But there are insufficient nurses with which to
staff the hospital and only limited services can be provided.

We could multiply these examples by the hundreds and see the
suffering, the sorrow, the tragedy of life in areas near and far from
here. These problems are not brought on because sin and trans-
gression are more common there than here. These people are not
handicapped by lack of intelligence, ability, or industry, but by
extreme poverty, lack of education, and insufficient opportunity.
How they reach out to us and ask, "Can you help us to enjoy the
blessings that you in America take for granted?"

Brethren, how do we solve these problems that exist in these
faraway places where the Church is growing more rapidly than in
other parts of the earth—in South and Central America, the islands
of the Pacific, and areas of Asia, where baptisms are not measured in
the tens or the hundreds, but in the thousands? These people come
into the Church and need our help. They need our assistance with
health and with every phase of life. What wonderful people they
are! You can't help but love them as you meet and talk with them.
You want to do something to reach out and lift them up and share
with them the blessings that we have in such great abundance. (*CR*,
October 1971, pp. 121-22.)

Health services missionaries have served in the bar-
rios of the Philippines, in the high Andes mountains of
Peru, and in the deserts of North America. They have
labored among Tongans, Italians, American Indians,
and Chinese. They have been sent to Thailand, Tahiti,
Bolivia, Hong Kong, Uruguay, Korea, Mexico, Samoa,
Guatemala, and many other nations. They have come
from such countries as Australia, Denmark, New Zealand, Canada, Chile, the United States, Switzerland,
Germany, England, Ireland, Taiwan, and Scotland.
Truly, this is brotherhood in action!

Three guiding principles have characterized the
Church's health program:

1. Appropriate existing community health resources
should be used by the Saints. Members of the Church
pay taxes to local, state, and federal governments, and
they contribute voluntarily to community fund-raising
projects. Therefore, they are entitled to receive care in
tax-supported or voluntary health facilities and government tax-supported health programs to which they have
contributed. Only those essential facilities and services

that are not provided locally or are not provided in consistency with eternal principles need become of concern to the Church. Members who live in countries that have adequate health facilities, doctors, and nurses should, in the spirit of brotherhood, help their brothers and sisters in lands where such facilities and personnel are not available.

2. Disease prevention should be emphasized in the Church's worldwide health efforts. The Word of Wisdom teaches good health maintenance and prevention of disease rather than how to cure sickness. Prevention is inexpensive when compared with the cost of professional health care. It is based on health education and prepares people to care for themselves.

3. Health services should be correlated through the established Church organization, as are other programs of the Church. When a member has a problem related to health, assistance can be obtained through a priesthood-correlated program.

Reports from missionaries who have served in the program are one of the best indicators of the program's success. Eileen Draper, who served in a remote Guatemalan village, wrote: "I feel that, through our efforts, ignorance was replaced by knowledge, truth took the place of tradition, understanding overcame fear, and hope now exists where despair once prevailed. Members now understand more about the causes of health problems and are better able to prevent or cope with them. What a thrill it was to see mothers learn to care for their children and wives to find that cooking on a simple stove was better than kneeling in the smoke from a fire built on the floor." (*Ensign,* December 1973, p. 65.)

Kathleen Stoddard and Florence Warren were greeted by a brass band and a welcome by the mayor when they arrived in the small Bolivian town of Tupiza. There they taught first aid and health practices, including artificial respiration, treatment of blisters and burns, emergency child delivery, hygiene, and nutrition. In Cochabamba, the second largest city in Bolivia, the largest theater in town was rented so the health course could be presented. Some four hundred persons attended the week-long course. (*Ensign,* September 1973, p. 72.)

Proselyting still occupies a prominent role in the labors of the health services missionary. But his proselyting is of a special quality. By the very nature of his professional competence, he is able to gain access to the professional people with whom he will work. Often he will work with government health officials, local surgeons, anesthetists, and dentists. It is only natural that in explaining his purpose in being in the country, he will also explain the Word of Wisdom, modern revelation, and how the Church was restored through the Prophet Joseph Smith.

As the missionaries meet with local groups, teaching them proper dental care, personal hygiene, or the importance of boiling their water before drinking it or preparing food with it, there are usually many present who are not members of the Church. Here, again, it is a simple matter to direct the discussion to religion, then direct interested persons to proselyting missionaries.

Margaret Anne Stubbs, who served in the Philippine Manila Mission, wrote about her proselyting activities in a report to the Church's health services department in December 1974:

This Monday was a very special day for us. We taught forty day-care nursery staff from the Social Welfare Department nutrition, using visual aids. Each day-care worker teaches sixty mothers. The lesson went across really well, and after we had finished, the doctor asked us, "Since you are here, why don't you tell us about your church." We were so happy. We told them about the Prophet and family home evening and about the health program. They asked us lots of questions. The Lord was really with us, as the answers just came out. I've never felt the Spirit so strongly as I did in that meeting. The director said, "I've always hidden when I have seen your elders, but next time I will invite them in, as I want to learn more about your church." Another person told us how she had read that Mormons have fewer cases of cancer. We were able to tell them that that is because we don't smoke or drink. The director's brother-in-law in the United States is a member. I have a strong feeling that if handled right and taken slowly, she will join the Church also. Just think how many people she affects! I don't think the elders will have any trouble getting into the homes of the day-care workers, as the Lord was really with us, and we left the people still having questions so they will be wanting to meet the missionaries.

Another health services missionary told about participating with the elders in a street display, where they were able to introduce people to the gospel through the Word of Wisdom. "We use a homemade smoking machine that shows what tars and nicotine do to the lungs of those who smoke. We take along some of our charts and visual aids and participate in explaining and answering questions. The elders get a lot of referrals this way."

Along with its concern for the health of the Saints in various areas of the world, the Church is also concerned with the health of the missionaries who are called to teach the gospel. In recent years the Church's health services agencies have participated with the Missionary Department in recommending measures to identify missionaries with potential health problems. Immunizations have been reviewed, and a schedule of immunizations adopted to meet all international health requirements as well as provide adequate protection for missionaries in the field. Through immunization with gamma globulin, for example, the number of missionaries infected with infectious hepatitis dropped in one year from over 170 to fewer than ten.

Another program that is carried out in some of the missions involves periodic testing of missionaries for exposure to tuberculosis. This has succeeded in alerting several missionaries to the possibility of tuberculosis infection where otherwise they might not have discovered the problem until the disease was present and perhaps far advanced.

Health education programs have been introduced in missions where parasitic diseases have often been a problem, and the incidence of dysentery among missionaries in one mission was reduced from 44 percent to nearly none. (James O. Mason, report to the General Priesthood Committee, September 1973.)

In support of the health services efforts, the Relief Society has been preparing family health lessons to educate the women of the Church on improved nutrition, prevention of disease, first aid, and home nursing. Special instructions are given on understanding diseases and their causes and transmission, cleanliness of food and kitchen, chronic diseases, physical fitness, weight control, dental hygiene, home accident prevention, and social and emotional illness.

"Assisting each member to reach his optimal physical and mental health is the health goal of the Church," the sisters are told, "and the home is where good health should begin." (*1974-75 Relief Society Courses of Study.*)

The health programs of the Church have initiated significant changes in the lives of many Latter-day Saints. Through it the health and well-being of Saints throughout the world have been noticeably influenced and improved, as they are coming closer to the goal outlined by the Lord in section 89 of the Doctrine and Covenants:

"And all saints who remember to keep and do these sayings, walking in obedience to the commandments, shall receive health in their navel and marrow to their bones;

"And shall find wisdom and great treasures of knowledge, even hidden treasures;

"And shall run and not be weary, and shall walk and not faint.

"And I, the Lord, give unto them a promise, that the destroying angel shall pass by them, as the children of Israel, and not slay them." (D&C 89:18-21.)

7

OPENING THE DOORS

In the late 1840s a small boy set out with his mother from Nauvoo, then a prosperous, handsome city on the Mississippi River flatlands below the bluffs of western Illinois. Nauvoo was a Mormon city, and the Mormons were being driven out by hostile neighbors. The boy was Peter Johnson. Born in Denmark, he had been brought to America and Nauvoo when very young, and now he was required to travel in a handcart company fifteen hundred miles more across the western American plains to what was to become the Territory of Utah. En route, the party with which Peter and his mother traveled was stranded by winter gales in Wyoming; only provisions rushed to them by Brigham Young saved their lives. But Peter Johnson prospered in Utah.

So did John Kennedy, a coal miner in Kilmarnock, Scotland, who as a young lad was converted to the Mormon faith by American missionaries. He immigrated to America and found a job in the coal mines of Almy, Wyoming. Later he became the first Mormon bishop of the small settlement of Kennedysville, Utah, later known as Argyle and then Randolph.

Peter Johnson and John Kennedy became partners and organized and founded the Bank of Randolph in northeastern Utah. But they were more than banking partners; they were also the grandfathers of David M. Kennedy, who was to become one of the most distinguished and widely traveled diplomats in the history of the Latter-day Saints. David would also hold the highest positions in the government of the United States of any other Mormon or any other person born in the State of Utah.

In finance, he became chairman of one of the world's largest banking institutions, the Continental Illinois National Bank and Trust Company of Chicago. In government, he became Secretary of the Treasury, the world's leading financial officer, ranking fourth in the line of succession to the Presidency of the United States. As a member of President Richard M. Nixon's cabinet, he ranked next to the Secretary of State and above the Deputy Undersecretary. In diplomacy he became U.S. Ambassador-at-Large and also served as United States Ambassador to the North Atlantic Treaty Organization (NATO) in Europe.

David Matthew Kennedy was born in Randolph, Utah, on July 21, 1905, a son of George and Katherine Johnson Kennedy. His father was a rancher, legislator, and state road superintendent. David spent his earliest years, and most of the summers after that, on the family's "Quarter Circle T" ranch. Until the fourth grade, when he moved with his mother to Kaysville, Utah, David attended school in Randolph. His mother was ill most of her life, and he was assigned to care for her, since there were only boys in the family and his four older brothers were needed to work on the ranch in Randolph. After two years in Kaysville, David and his mother moved to Ogden, in order to be more convenient to doctors and medical help.

He worked most of the time during his high school years, despite the fact that his father was a successful and substantial rancher. During these high school years David was looking forward to filling a proselyting mission for the Church, and at nineteen he thought it was strange that he had not received a call. He had saved more than $1,000 in the local bank for that purpose. But since no call came, he made plans to marry Lenora Bingham of Ogden. The wedding announcements were already printed when his bishop approached him with the proposal that he should accept a call as a fulltime missionary for the Church, telling him, "You go ahead and get married, then you can leave for the mission field."

David's and Lenora's parents agreed. The couple were married in the Salt Lake Temple in November 1924, and he left in January for his mission to England. He spent all of his mission in Liverpool, at 295 Edge Lane, the mission headquarters, serving under two mission presidents, James E. Talmage and John A. Widtsoe.

After his mission, David and Lenora decided to move to Washington, D.C., where he earned an M.A. degree in 1935 and an LL.B. degree in 1947, both from George Washington University. He also pursued his interest in banking at the Stonier Graduate School of Banking at Rutgers University, from which he was graduated in 1939.

David Kennedy worked for sixteen years for the Federal Reserve System, where he acquired a broad knowledge of money markets. Sought out by several New York City banks, he finally decided to accept an offer from the Continental Illinois Bank. He became a full vice-president of the bank in 1951, and was elected president in 1956. His tenure as head of Continental Illinois brought vast changes to that institution; in the words of one observer, he "peeled the starch off." It was no doubt his great success in introducing vigorous, innovative programs, and particularly the bank's expansion of overseas services, that led to his appointment as U.S. Secretary of the Treasury in 1969, a position he held until 1971.

Though David Kennedy retired from government service in March 1973, during that year alone he flew back and forth between Europe and Washington, D.C.,

thirty-nine times; traveled to all but two of the NATO
countries, visiting some of them several times; made
three official visits to Portugal; and was involved in ne-
gotiations in Spain.

Thus it was as a capstone to a distinguished career in
international affairs that David Kennedy was called to
serve as a special representative of the First Presidency of
The Church of Jesus Christ of Latter-day Saints in April
1974.

During the night before he was scheduled to meet
with the First Presidency about this new calling, he
prayerfully reflected upon the prospect of serving as an
ambassador-at-large for the prophet and the people of
God. He thought about how he could assist the Church
in opening up new countries for missionary work and
strengthening its position worldwide. And, he recalls, he
wondered why he—and not others whom he thought
of—might be called to take such an assignment. But
when he entered President Spencer W. Kimball's office
the next morning, he was greeted warmly and, in Elder
Kennedy's words, "Without a chance for me to defend
myself, President Kimball took my hand and simply
said, 'We would like you to serve the Lord in this new
capacity as our special representative. Are you willing to
serve?' "

David Kennedy replied, "I've said 'no' to many
people in my life. I've been taught to say no to the
world, but I can't say no to the prophet of the Lord.
Whatever you ask me to do I'll do, if I can."

President Kimball told him that in this job he would
be a specialist in helping to open new countries for
teaching the gospel and advising the First Presidency on
how to strengthen the Church in new areas.

"I'll do my best," Elder Kennedy replied. Then he
added, "But I want to say that in time you will need
younger men to carry out this work. We must keep current, and new people will have to be asked to help carry
forward the work. Also, in every country we must make
a contribution, not just ask for favors all the time."

On April 4, 1974, President Kimball elaborated

upon the urgent need for the Church to build bridges between the known and unknown--that the gospel of Christ must literally cover the earth. In an address to Regional Representatives of the Twelve he remarked:

> The Twelve have the keys and those they send have the command to open doors. Today we are blessed with many strong, trained men, in government, in foreign service, and with much prestige and "know-how." Perhaps we can bring to our call men like those who can make new contacts with emperors and kings and rulers and magistrates. . . .
>
> I believe the Lord can do anything he sets his mind to do. But I see no good reason why the Lord would open doors that we are not prepared to enter. Why should he break down the Iron Curtain or the Bamboo Curtain or any other curtain if we are still unprepared to enter?
>
> I believe we have men who could help the apostles to open these doors--statesmen, able and trustworthy--but, when we are ready for them. (*Ensign*, October 1974, pp. 6, 7.)

In that same meeting, President Kimball introduced David Kennedy as an early agent in that coming enterprise. On July 24, 1975, Brother Kennedy received the following letter from President Kimball:

> Dear Brother Kennedy:
>
> As I ran across this statement in the Doctrine and Covenants, I resolved to call upon every mission and stake and every ward and branch and every family and individual to pray for you and us as we approached the countries that are "locked" in and in which we have not yet found favor.
>
> We pray for you especially in your important work.
>
> The scripture reads: "And again, I say unto you, that whosoever ye shall send in my name, by the voice of your brethren, the Twelve, duly recommended and authorized by you, shall have power to open the door of my kingdom *unto any nation whithersoever ye shall send them.*" (D&C 112:21.)
>
> And so in our home, we pray in every prayer for the Lord to open the gates.
>
> With our sincere thanks and affection.
>
> Faithfully yours,
> Spencer W. Kimball
> President

Since his appointment as ambassador-at-large for the Church, David Kennedy has traveled the earth many times over in efforts to break new ground and in seeking

official recognition for the Church in many lands. He
has also accompanied the president of the Church in
official visits with heads of state and high government
officials. Inspired and inspirational gains have been
made. He has been instrumental in gaining recognition
and legal admission in some—Portugal in 1974 and Po-
land in 1977, for example—and has been successful in
furthering the interests of the Church in many others.

In countries where public street meetings and door-
to-door tracting are not allowed, he has suggested the
need for adjustments in missionary work; and he has
repeatedly urged Latter-day Saints to become more active, resourceful, and realistic in helping solve problems
facing the Church in the nations of the earth. Although
he has not minimized the obstacles standing in the way
of further Church expansion, he ardently reflects the
confidence of the First Presidency and the Council of the
Twelve that The Church of Jesus Christ of Latter-day
Saints will continue to roll forth even to "the nethermost
parts of the earth." David M. Kennedy has now become
a living symbol of a widespread Mormon commitment—
that all countries now closed will yet open their doors
and allow the Church to bring in the message of the restored gospel of Jesus Christ.

8

MORE NATIONS THAN ONE

by David M. Kennedy

(Note: In a spirit of instruction and admonition the Lord revealed to the prophet Nephi that foolish gentiles in the latter days would be reluctant to see His hand-dealings on a more comprehensive scale, and thus He fervently asked: "Know ye not that there are more nations than one? Know ye not that I, the Lord your God have created all men. . . ?" [2 Nephi 29:7.] The implications of belonging to an expanding, universalizing church are wide ranging. Some are political, and it is of these that David M. Kennedy speaks here, as he reflects upon his labors among the nations of the earth as a special representative of the Church. His comments are based on interviews conducted in Salt Lake City during a three-year period ending in 1977.)

I feel no fundamental conflict between my commitment as a Latter-day Saint and my commitment as a citizen of the United States. I would hope that other members of the Church in other countries would also be able to be fully committed to the gospel and yet live as patriotic citizens of their respective countries.

In the United States, we have a system of government that provides police protection against

violence, robbery, and personal injury, and that enforces
the laws and requires the compliance of the people in
matters of public security. We have certain kinds of
restraints in our country, and the citizens of any country
must expect some of these to a greater or lesser degree.

We now have Church members and missionaries
living in many countries. Some of these countries have
strongly centralized governments, even totalitarian
forms of government; some are democracies; some are
socialist; some are communist. In terms of the gospel, the
prime consideration is the free agency of man.

So long as the government permits me to attend
church; so long as it permits me to get on my knees in
prayer; so long as it permits me to be baptized for the
remission of my sins; so long as it permits me to partake
of the sacrament of the Lord's supper and to obey the
commandments of the Lord; so long as the government
does not force me to commit crime; so long as I am not
required to live separately from my wife and children—I
can live as a Latter-day Saint within that political
system. As an individual I may wish to seek reforms in
the system, but I have no right to say that that comes
from my membership in the Church, or I cannot do that
in the name of the Church.

I frequently walk down the streets of the cities of
Eastern Europe and elsewhere. The people there point
out to me that they are also free to move about, that
they are also protected from criminals, that they too
mingle and sing in the parks, that they also smile and
are happy. And I believe this is generally true. One can
see that. Yes, there are agitators in these countries. But
I've met hotel clerks, porters, chauffeurs, people in
restaurants and on the streets, and almost all of them are
kind and friendly. They are no different from people in
other countries. Their systems of government are
different, but I see no reason why good Latter-day Saints
cannot live under a variety of political and economic
systems.

Sometimes I find people not happy with their
working conditions. Well, a lot of people in America are

not happy with their working conditions either. When I
was young, it was very hard to get a job. We would work
at anything. Electricians, plumbers, and carpenters
would be willing to dig ditches. They would be willing
to clerk in stores. But there was very little work
available. Now, of course, they are not willing to work
other than in their own trades or fields; labor in the
United States is all specialized, compartmentalized.

Attitudes in the world are changing. In part because
of tourism and rapid transportation we are seeing others
more intimately than before; foreigners are seeing our
way of life—not only the leaders, but the people
generally are much more aware of conditions in the
world. They are thinking and evaluating now as never
before. Their expectations are much higher. In
communist countries, as in some other lands, there are
people who want to dominate and control the public. So
somebody makes a case that because we Latter-day
Saints believe in free agency, we should not even talk
with them, we should not have any discourse or trade
with them, we should not have anything to do with
them. That's one philosophy that has been advocated
widely in the United States.

I take the position that all people on earth are
children of our Father in heaven. By pre-earth
assignment or by chance, or for some other reason, we
have all been born in particular places. I can't really
explain that. But having been born in their respective
countries, why should all people not be entitled to any
truth they can get? If we have truth—and we do—they
are entitled to it. So we are responsible to make it
available to them. The truth does have a great impact
and a good influence on the thinking of people, and with
it they are encouraged to improve their lives. But it is
not intended to create a forceful revolutionary
movement of any kind. These governments simply will
not change drastically overnight, and our members are
not expected to be involved in efforts to bring this about.

It is of special interest to me that the gospel is now
moving into Hindu, Buddhist, and Muslim countries. I

am not sure what this implies in terms of the traditional thinking and beliefs of the people concerning religion. But there are people in the communist world who say they simply don't believe in God. There are such people in the United States. The Church must teach all these people the gospel of Jesus Christ. Surely they are entitled to hear the truth. Basically we must win them by our actions. Mormonism is not simply a few ideas here and there. It's a complete way of life, and that's our strength.

If Mormons are following their teachings, they are reaching out to help their fellowmen—the man next door as well as the brother who lives in a distant land.

One thing that concerns me as we become more successful and attract more members is that we keep a clear separation of church and state. The history of the Church in Nauvoo is in part a question of the non-Mormons' concern for the political power of the Church. This could yet be a force to be reckoned with and could become a disconcerting problem in some areas of the world because basically, Latter-day Saints have heretofore lived in democracies. We believe in common consent as an eternal principle. Since there are ways in which the American secular or political culture is in full agreement with the gospel and some ways in which they do not agree, it is important to maintain a distinction between church and state in the U.S. as elsewhere in the world. Yet as a church we have practically owed our life to the safeguards of the government of the United States.

With regard to the Constitution of the United States, it is the principles found therein that we ought to talk about. As long as the principles of the Constitution are upheld, the government will be secure. The Constitution calls for religious freedom, but the Mormons were persecuted in the United States about as much as they were anywhere else in the world. The Prophet Joseph Smith was killed within the framework of the American political system, but contrary to constitutional principles. The Church could be established in the United States because of inspired constitutional

principles, but the government and political system has
not always been ideal. We know that America is a choice
land and that the basic principles of the U.S.
Constitution are eternal, but we cannot carry this much
further without meeting some justifiable arguments.
And this comes up from time to time in my discussions
with different peoples abroad.

Certainly America is a blessed land. Look at its
resources. Look at what it has done. And I believe it will
continue to be blessed as long as the people are doing
what they should be doing. The Lord gives blessings
when people obey him and he takes them away when
people disobey. To that same extent I say to members of
the Church in other countries, you and your fellow
countrymen will be blessed in accordance with your
obedience to the commandments of the Lord. But there
is something more to it than this. Americans must be
very careful not to give the impression that they are
better or more righteous than others simply because they
are Americans. And I assume the same can be said of
people in other nations.

During a meeting with the press at the time of the
Asia area general conference, I was asked by a reporter
in Tokyo about Mormonism and politics. He said, "You
believe in being 'subject to kings, presidents, rulers,
magistrates, in honoring, obeying, and sustaining the
law.' But what happens when the government passes a
law that disagrees with the teachings of your church?
What do you do? Do you tell your people to ignore the
teachings of the Church and follow the laws of the
land?" Now, there was more to this question than met
the eye. He was thinking of communist China at the
time.

I gave an outspoken response. I knew that he was
planning to say in the press that he had asked this
question of the Mormon prophet (he had asked
President Kimball this question, and the President
deferred to me), and that if he implied that they could
ignore Church teachings, he could be accused of
misleading the members of the Church. If he gave the

impression that the President refused to respond to such a question, he would say that he didn't really believe in honoring, obeying, and sustaining the law. Either way, we would be in trouble.

So I said the following to him:

"We believe in God the Eternal Father and in Jesus Christ, his Son. We believe that Jesus is the Redeemer of the world, that he carried out an atoning sacrifice, and that he was crucified for the sins of man to make it possible for the redemption of man. We believe in baptism by immersion for the remission of sins. We also believe in the Holy Ghost and in the laying on of hands for all these gifts. And we believe in authority from God, the priesthood, which is the power to act and function in his name. These are our basic beliefs. But we also believe in the eternal relationship of marriage. We believe in the resurrection from the dead. These are fundamental Mormon beliefs on which there is no compromise. One cannot be a faithful Latter-day Saint unless he believes in these great truths. Now we can put these on the one side.

"On the other hand, we believe in being subject to kings, presidents, rulers, and magistrates because we believe there must be order in society. People must have opportunity to associate; they must have protection. Men do not ordinarily live alone in isolation, so laws must be set up for the benefit of man. And human beings do not set up these social and political regulations in the same way everywhere. Each group of people in a room will set up its government differently. They will devise their own street, utility, health, and food regulations. Somebody has to pay for these, so they usually have a tax system.

"So Latter-day Saints say, 'Render unto Caesar the things that are Caesar's; and to God the things that are God's,' as Jesus explained to the Pharisees. The two have to be separated.

"Some governments pass laws that we as individual Latter-day Saints may not like, but the Church does not usually take a stand on such matters. That is up to the

individual citizens of that country, whether they are
members or not. Latter-day Saints, like other citizens of
a country, are entitled to express their own views,
whether popular or unpopular. They can bring about
change within the system by an orderly process. In the
United States most members of The Church of Jesus
Christ of Latter-day Saints are Democrats or
Republicans. I'm a Republican. But there are many
good members in both political parties."

I gave this response in Japan among a people who
have lived under an emperor for many hundreds of
years. In some countries, as in Latin America, the people
cannot be expected to follow the U.S. form of
government and survive. Eventually they may want to,
but at present they cannot. Revolutions and revolts are
rather common in that part of the world, as in some
places in Asia. In the Book of Mormon there were
benevolent kings and rulers and there were also
disreputable kings. A queen reigns over the British
people and over Latter-day Saints living in her realm.
The emperor of Japan and the king of Thailand both
have members of the Church under their jurisdiction.

The Church is now established in countries with
different kinds of histories, different systems of
economics and politics, and different ways of life. In
Saudi Arabia, Faisal was a man of strong religious
beliefs, and with tremendous power to maintain order in
that country. Now I do not believe that we have to judge
whether that is all good or all bad. Our concern should
be whether the teachings of the gospel are allowed to
flourish or whether the people are forced to follow
immoral or ungodly practices. If the heads of
governments allow the people to believe in God and
these other fundamental teachings I enumerated to the
Japanese newspaper reporter, that's all we can ask for.
We simply cannot expect to agitate for peripheral
things.

As an example, if one talks about free enterprise he
has to make qualifications. Every government, including
that of the United States, has various economic

regulations. We have regulations in utilities, banking, airlines, and in many other fields. To suggest that all this is a divine economic system raises serious questions in the minds of some.

I think the only really divine system was revealed by the Lord in the United Order, but we have not yet learned how to live that. The Lord's plan calls for unselfishness and service. It calls for a willingness to give. We Mormons have not yet been able to live these principles to the full. We have tithing to carry us over in the meantime. Even with the principles of tithing the Church faces administrative difficulties in some countries. There are restrictions in spending funds and in transmitting them across national boundaries.

Now I would like to make a few comments about the Arab world as a prospective mission field for The Church of Jesus Christ of Latter-day Saints. We have members in Iran, and we have missionaries in other Muslim countries. We have been in Lebanon, we are now in Indonesia, and I would hope we could establish the Church in Egypt and other countries before too long. This will present many problems. Sometimes writers and tourists in the Church tend to work against missionary prospects in Muslim countries. Stated simply, the recurring problem is the apparent attitude among some Latter-day Saint members, tourists, students, editors, and teachers who speak out irresponsibly in favor of the political aims and activities of the state of Israel in opposition to the Arab countries. These sometimes strident utterances tend to cause repercussions in countries such as Egypt, Iran, Lebanon, and Saudi Arabia. We should all do what we can to stop prejudicial publications and speeches. I'd like to see at least one balanced article by good members of the Church in treatment of the Muslims.

One of the most difficult discussions I have ever had on this problem was with a member of my own family some years ago. I had just returned from Egypt, where I had spent four hours with President Nasser just before the June war of 1967. He was giving his views of Israel. I asked him why he was taking such a stern attitude.

"Well, I'm getting blamed by your State Department. I'm blamed by everyone for causing the trouble between Egypt and Israel. But I want to say this is not Nasser. These disputes have been going on for hundreds of years.

"They're taking our territory. Israel's a very progressive group of people. Many of the Jews are businessmen. You know that. There are Jews in every country of the world. You have many of them in the United States. They're good people. Sincerely, we like them. We have no trouble with the Jews. Our fight is with Israel because that state wants more and more of our land. When will it stop its desire for expansion? With all of their productive ability, and all the funds they are getting from all over the world, and with their campaign to bring more and more people into their country, they will continue to want more and more territory. How can anyone expect us to sit here and let this government expand uncontested?"

What we are dealing with here is not a simple matter. I've never read anything in any of the standard works that says that political or military leaders have necessarily been divinely appointed to their jobs, or even that the present nation of Israel is inevitably divine.

My message is that we should stand by the prophecies and promises of the Lord—all of them, not just some. And in supporting one nation against another, who is always capable of saying what is right? What we want is righteousness. We want it among the Arabs and we want it among the Jews. We admire the Jews, and if they will accept the gospel we will rejoice. So far, they have shown no greater disposition to embrace the gospel and worship the Savior than have the Arabs.

I had an interesting experience on this very thing. I was in Athens with Ted Kollek, the mayor of Jerusalem. At the time he was in the cabinet of Levi Eshkol, the prime minister who followed Ben Gurion. I had given a dinner in Chicago that Eshkol and other members of his cabinet attended. Ted had visited Chicago a number of

times, so I was already acquainted with him. Lenora, my
wife, Ted Kollek, and I also visited the Museum of
Antiquity in Athens together and I found him
well-versed in history and customs. It was an enjoyable
experience with a very able and well-informed person.

On that occasion, Kollek commented, "I understand
you're a Mormon. Do you know that one of your
early-day prophets prophesied about Israel? He told it
just as it is today."

"Is that right?"

"Yes. And let me quote to you from his prayer."
After doing so, he asked: "Would you like to have a
copy?"

"I'd like that very much."

I didn't tell him that the Orson Hyde prayer was
well known among the Mormon people.

So he later sent me both a Hebrew language and an
English language translation of Elder Hyde's prayer. I
used that in a Jewish fund-raising dinner. I hadn't
expected to give a speech because I had been told there
would be none. But there were several important Jewish
speakers at the dinner, and they were eloquent orators.
Some of them were heaping praise on me so I felt
constrained to say something in response. On the spur of
the moment I felt constrained to give a Mormon sermon.
I told the two thousand guests about receiving the Orson
Hyde prayer from Ted Kollek, the mayor of Jerusalem.
Of course he's a great Jewish leader, and when I told
them the story of Orson Hyde they were all amazed and
aghast. Afterwards many people came up asking
questions about the prayer and wanting copies. I gave
out copies and promises of copies that night.

Ted Kollek sent me a copy of a book he has written
on Jerusalem. When President Harold B. Lee was
planning his trip to the Holy Land in 1972, I called Ted
at his home in Jerusalem, told him the president of the
Church was coming over, and asked him if he would be
kind enough to receive him and take care of him. And he
did. He called me afterwards and said he very much
enjoyed meeting President Lee.

I am very fond of the Jewish people. I know they are a people of great promise. I'm on their side also. Indeed, I have little problem in the countries of the Middle East because they know I deal fairly with all of them. I learned the need for this earlier in my bank work. We must learn to be impartial to all and to accept people on their individual merits wherever they may live. This conflict between the Arab and Jewish worlds is just one of many with which the Church must wait ultimately for solution, as only then can we carry the restored gospel into all lands.

II
UNTO THE EUROPEANS

9

THE UPSURGE OF
AN ALPINE FAMILY

Karl Ringger is an unusual man. He is thoroughly Swiss, but he is also typical of many other Europeans who joined The Church of Jesus Christ of Latter-day Saints at the beginning of the twentieth century. He typifies a person who became caught between allegiance to a church that was primarily American, but that in his mind was also a universal faith. The experiences of the Ringger family are typical of those of many converts in Paris, Berlin, Amsterdam, and other parts of Europe. Many of these converts, influenced by their faith in the restored gospel, have risen from lower class status and worked their way up to positions of economic, social, educational, and religious leadership. Through membership in the Church they have been able to transcend their former position and achieve in their employment and communities.

The story begins with Elizabeth Zobeli, Karl's mother. A humble, uneducated widow, she earned her livelihood taking odd jobs as a cleaning lady in Zurich. In fact, she was a house servant for the Mormon missionaries, and became the first of her family to join the

Church. But it has been through her son Karl that the
rise of the Ringger family has evolved. He is the decisive force that has allowed his immediate posterity to
have the new, improved quality of life they now enjoy.

Within three generations descendants of Elizabeth
Zobeli have become thriving leaders of business, industry, and church not only in Switzerland, but also in
various parts of the United States. They have built a
new interrelationship between their European homeland
and their adopted land of America. Missionary grand-
sons of Brother Ringger have served with distinction in
Austria, Germany, and other countries of Europe. Because of their family background, they have been able to
speak German with considerable fluency and accuracy,
but they regard themselves as native Americans. In this,
the Ringgers have become a microcosm of Mormon
convert families throughout the world.

The Swiss people are not only politically democratic,
but also fiercely proud of their individuality. They
cherish the idea of political responsibility, but rather
than having government do things for them, they prefer
independence in deciding the important issues of their
lives. Unlike many nations of Europe, the Swiss have no
titled citizens left over from traditional kingdoms and
empires. Economic position and skill in a trade or
profession, not descent from a particular bloodline, determine social class.

The Ringger family came from the working class
background that was typical of converts to the Church
in the early days of this century. Karl was a factory
worker, a machinist. When he lost that job, he turned to
salesmanship, and slowly worked himself up to a higher
economic level. Through a blending of religious faith
and enterprising tenacity, he was able to pay tithing and
also improve upon his financial holdings and security.

In the countries of Europe at the time of Karl's baptism, particularly among people of higher educational
achievement, American culture was looked down upon.
The Church itself was regarded as a sect, always a more
negative concept in Europe than in the United States.

Yet here was a man who cheerfully and wholeheartedly accepted the so-called disadvantages that were then attached to membership in the Church by the Europeans.

After the beginning of World War I, European countries with nationalistic leanings continued to share this feeling of condescension toward American culture; yet among many of the European working class, America was regarded as the attractive symbol of a better world. It was this ambivalent view of the United States that intensified the question in the minds of many European converts of whether they should indeed gather to the Zion in the American West. What should they give up and what should they keep of their earlier lives? Should they remain European or should they go to America? Were they good Saints if they went, or should they stay?

These were some of the questions the Ringger family asked themselves. Karl was more cosmopolitan than many European converts, but he was also very proud of being Swiss. His cosmopolitan attitude influenced his desire to learn foreign languages, particularly English. He eagerly learned English from missionaries, French while serving in the army in Paris, and Italian while assigned to a military unit in an Italian-speaking region of Switzerland. He became interested in learning about many subjects, and his membership in the Church, which teaches that one should "seek learning, even by study and also by faith" (D&C 88:118), led him to expand his knowledge and scholarship. Few others among the Saints in Europe could match his knowledge of the Bible. When authorities of the Church visited Europe, those Europeans who spoke English had special opportunities to serve, and Karl was especially blessed in being able to meet and converse with these leaders.

Brother Ringger was called to be the first Latter-day Saint patriarch in Europe. Finnish, Swedish, Dutch, and other Saints often conversed with him in English, while his command of German, French, and Italian enabled him to communicate with members from most of the major European countries who came to receive blessings and to visit the temple near Bern.

Karl Ringger is fiercely individualistic. He was reared in a European community that has had difficulty understanding the doctrines of consensus and compromise so distinctly characteristic of The Church of Jesus Christ of Latter-day Saints. A German proverb says, "*Wem Gott ein Amt gibt, gibt er auch den Verstand*"—— "To whom God gives a position [of authority] he also gives understanding." Leadership implies sternness and authoritarianism in certain European cultures. In the early days of the Church in Europe, the leader was thought to be responsible for carrying the load. Such concepts have substantially changed in recent years, but they are repeatedly suggested in Brother Ringger's descriptions of life among first-generation Latter-day Saints in Switzerland.

The story of Mormonism in Europe is partially told in the lives of Karl and Maria Ringger, who represent numerous converts of their generation in Europe. It is also reflected, to a degree, in the lives of their children, the second generation. Two of their sons and a daughter have remained in Switzerland.

Two of their daughters have immigrated to America, and they reside in Salt Lake City and in Atlanta, Georgia, respectively. It is through the reminiscences of the other two sons, Louis and Carl, who also immigrated to America, that the story of the Ringger family is brought up to contemporary times. These comments on Swiss perceptions of American missionaries and of problems of adapting Church programs in Switzerland, as well as in the early days of the Church in Switzerland as viewed by young second-generation natives, add a new dimension to the processes of Church growth in Europe today.

Louis Ringger gives much of the credit for his success in life to the Church. An engineer, he holds a major executive position with the U.S. Steel Corporation in Provo, Utah. He has been active in civic and community organizations, including the Boy Scouts of America, the Utah National Parks Council, the United Way, and the Association of Iron and Steel Engineers. In the Church he has been a bishop and a high councilor. He and his wife, Hilde, are the parents of three sons and one daughter, all graduates of Brigham Young University.

Carl, the eldest Ringger son, struggled for many years in deciding on a vocation before leaving his native land. In the United States he found employment at the Geneva Division of United States Steel Corporation in Utah, where in time he rose to the position of maintenance foreman. He also has been active in the community and church, and has served as a counselor in the presidency of the Pleasant Grove Stake.

In the chapters that follow, based on interviews with members of the Ringger family, the contrast between the struggles of a first-generation European, Karl Ringger, and those of his sons, of the second generation, reflect many of the struggles and problems faced by Latter-day Saints in Europe or who come from European backgrounds.

10
KARL RINGGER'S STORY

My mother, Elisabeth Zobeli, was born July 19, 1853, in Niederweingen, Switzerland, a small farming town about twenty miles from Zurich. She was the oldest daughter of seven children. She was only twelve years old when her father told her, "When I come home this evening, I don't expect to see you here any more." So she hired out as a domestic for five Swiss francs per month. At fourteen years of age she went to work in a textile mill in Killwangen, where she earned nine francs every two weeks, which was the amount she had to pay for board and room. Later she worked for many years as a maid in a home near Wangen.

In 1889, when Mother was thirty-six years old, she married my father in Zurich. Within a year a little daughter was born, but the baby died two months later. I was born in 1891, and my father died when I was fifteen months old, reportedly of lung cancer.

Father was a very colorful person who learned the trade of a tile layer and traveled for a time as a journeyman roofer. Later he found a job as a guard at the old Otenbach Prison in Zurich, which is why his trade appears in a civil register as a sheriff ranger. After the prison was closed, he went to work as a foreman in the freight department of the National Railroad. This, I think, contributed to his death at forty years of age, because in those days the air in and around freight yards was often full of black, irritating smoke.

After Father's death, Mother had to face a new life, a great struggle, to care for herself and me. Her widowhood lasted for sixty-three years, until she died at the age of 102.

Three years after Father's death Mother rented a room next to an apartment occupied by another widow. This lady left her room every Sunday morning at nine o'clock. One day in 1895 Mother asked her, "Where do you go every Sunday morning?" The woman answered, "Where? To the Mormons." She was a member of The Church of Jesus Christ of Latter-day Saints but had never disclosed it. Her name was Marie Bolliger. She invited Mother to go along with her but Mother refused, for she was a very independent person in all her decisions.

One day, however, she followed Mrs. Bolliger to the Mormon meeting place in Zurich. She told me later that during her first visit she said to herself, "This is my place. This is where I belong." Her positive conviction never faltered from that time on, though it was several years before she was baptized. After she became interested in the Church she had a difficult time with her sisters, who belonged to the Methodists; they gave her considerable opposition. Mother herself had belonged to the Swiss Reformed Church, but she had not been active. Her long working days didn't leave her any time for church. Interestingly, she was never visited during her whole widowhood by a minister or pastor of her church. Without such contacts, she kept struggling ahead on her own.

One incident concerning my mother had a decisive influence on my entire life. One evening I overheard her praying; she said, "Father, I am a poor widow, and I have nothing on this earth but my son. Please keep him

for me." This prayer was uttered just before she put me
in the Pestalozzi Home for Boys. Needless to say, I was
deeply touched.

Mother thought the right thing was to put me in the
home. I was six years old, and I remained there for ten
years. The boys in the home were orphans, part-orphans,
or boys from families with very limited means. All of
them were from somewhat the same social background,
where working parents had little time for them. It was a
good school, though it was very strict, without love. For
example, whenever one of the boys was punished, it was
done in front of the other forty boys. Although we were
very small, we had to herd cattle in the wet grass early in
the morning. My feeling was that my mother had made
a mistake to put me there because on the whole I was
raised without love. But she visited me the first Sunday
of each month.

At the Pestalozzi Home I had all kinds of
experiences, including a good deal of arbitrary
punishment. A new director, who was an excellent
teacher, took over while I was in the first grade. His
name was Herman Burer. He was a wonderful human
being. There were four of us boys in the first grade. He
put two of us on his knees and the other two directly in
front of him. That's the way he taught, and that's the
way I completed the first, second, and third grades.
When I was eleven years old I finished the sixth grade,
thanks to the personal attention of this teacher. But
school rules would not permit me to graduate until I was
twelve, so I had to sit for another year in the sixth grade.

When I was fifteen years old we boys had to work in
the garden. I was quite a loner, and the other boys
enjoyed teasing me. Once their teasing made me so
angry that I took a bean pole and ran after a boy who
had called me a name. The sharp stick pierced his foot,
broke, and remained sticking there. Master Burer said to
me, "Karl, I really should punish you, but I believe it
would be better if I give you the opportunity tonight
after the evening meal to walk around the big meadow.
Then you talk with the One up there and ask him to

help you overcome your disposition to become so easily angered. The way you are going now, you may end up in prison later in life. Now go outside and think about this." Of course, the One he had reference to was Heavenly Father.

After my sheltered stay at the home I went out into the world as a rather naive young man, forced to compete in the real world without any previous experience. I had had no connection with the opposite sex, for our teachers were men. So you could say that everything I learned from that point on I had to teach myself. First, I had to take stock of the world.

I departed from school with a small suitcase and caught the train for the village of Weisslingen, where I was to be apprenticed to a master machinist. I carried my bag for two miles up a hill and introduced myself to my new master. He put me in a room right beneath the roof. "Put your things away. Here is your closet. You sleep here. To eat, you come down to the kitchen." This is how my life developed. I never had the privilege of entering my master's living room, except to say hello and hand him my papers. This went on for three and a half years. I could not come and go as I pleased, and as an apprentice I earned no money. I had no opportunity to attend the LDS Church, so in due time I was confirmed in the Swiss Reformed Church and went to services on Sunday. Sometimes the other young apprentices in the congregation and I were permitted to help the custodian ring the bells.

Later on, when I had more freedom, I met with other young men in the village. Those who had money spent it on beer, while those of us who didn't have any money went for walks and developed a comradeship with one another. Later we were invited to join a local gymnastics club. At first I had an inferiority complex that was difficult to overcome. Finally I became a bit more forward, and eventually I gained self-confidence and the respect of others; I also learned to enjoy my trade.

When I was a small child, Mother had taken me along to meetings of the Church. But while I was at the

Pestalozzi Home, I had no contact with the Church. The
Swiss Church meant nothing to me, and because I let
my views be known, I was scorned and ostracized. My
mother had to suffer too, for when she visited me at
school, she was on the receiving end of slighting remarks.

As soon as I established contact with the Church in
Zurich after I finished my apprenticeship, the district
president, a Brother Manning, talked to Mother and me.
He said, "It is now time that you two believers consider
baptism." "Good," we agreed. "We will meet the elders
tomorrow." So we were finally baptized in the River
Sihl, after a thunderstorm, on June 16, 1912. Because of
the thunderstorm, the river was high and dirty.
However, I still had the feeling that our sins were all
washed away. I wanted to embrace the whole world, for
I had never felt so free and content. Mother, who was
baptized first, was also exultant.

During all this time Mother washed and scrubbed
for a living. She cleaned the meeting hall for the Church
for twenty-two years. During her life she had contact
with missionaries who later became General Authorities.
One whose name comes readily to mind was Levi Edgar
Young, who served as a district president and later
became a member of the First Council of the Seventy. At
another time the missionaries had rented an apartment
and Mother sublet a room from them. She took care of
their washing and cooked for them. Among the
missionaries was Brother Albert E. Bowen, who later was
ordained an apostle. President Henry D. Moyle of the
First Presidency served a mission in Switzerland early in
the present century.

Toward the end of my apprenticeship I met my wife-
to-be. In the village I took part in plays, and Marie Reif
sang in the women's choir that supported us. Her father
was the power-station attendant at the textile mill. The
Reifs were simple and charming people who greatly
impressed me. Marie seemed to me an angel, and
remained an angel all our life together. Toward the end
of my apprenticeship she started washing and mending
my shirts and socks. She even made me a new white

shirt. It was then that I knew she would someday become my wife.

I completed my apprenticeship in three and a half years and went to the trade school in Winterthur to take the examination and demonstrate practical knowledge. Then I worked half a year as a journeyman with the same master under whom I had served my apprenticeship. I was now earning the meager wage of 25 francs per month with board and room. Next I went to work in the steam turbine department of Brown Boveri, a large electrical firm. After working there for one year, 1911-12, I joined Escher-Wyss, in the ship construction division.

As I was still not married at that time, I told Mother that it was not right for me to consider myself settled. "I think I should go abroad to eat some other bread," I explained. Accordingly, in the spring of 1913 I left for Paris with a friend who worked with me at Escher-Wyss. During the fourteen days that we looked for work we slept in a Swiss hostel. I finally found work in a sheet-metal mill works. I remained there for a year, a prosperous and happy year for me.

Rather than associating with the Swiss nationals in Paris, I looked for the Mormon missionaries. I went to the Rue Faubourg du Temple, where the elders had their meeting place. I had been in Paris for three months by then, and knew where the meeting hall was, but at first I hadn't known any French. Assuming the American missionaries didn't know German, I learned French before going to meet them. Because I had prepared my testimony in French, I bore it on that Sunday. From then on I attended meetings every Sunday.

On Sunday mornings French farmers held an outdoor market outside our meeting place, with vegetables and fruit laid out on the ground on blankets. Upstairs we sang hymns and hoped that some of the shoppers would visit us. Later the elders found a different meeting hall in the Grenoble Quarter, near their apartment. On rainy Sunday afternoons, after the

formal meetings were over, we sang quartets. We had a
wonderful time. We sang so well together that when we
opened the window, the whole neighborhood opened
their windows also. Sometimes we heard *"Qui chante là-
haut? C'est beau.* (Who is singing up there? It is
beautiful.)" On Sundays when the weather was good, we
went for walks to Fontainebleau, Saint-Cloud, and some
of the parks of Paris.

After a year I left my position with the sheet-metal
firm. I didn't like the company because the Swiss
workers were all too jealous of each other and didn't
enjoy one another's advancements. I wrote to many
potential employers and one responded––a supplier of
auxiliary machines to the French War Ministry. I
enjoyed the work there very much. I earned twice as
much as before, and in a short time I could send 700
Swiss francs [$135] back to my mother. Although the
money was intended for her, she didn't use it. She
preferred to take care of herself, and she put all the
money into a savings account. This came in handy when
the war broke out and I had to return home.

In Paris I began to concern myself with politics. I
read the French newspapers and became well
acquainted with European politics, although I was only
twenty-three at the time. I asked myself, "Is France ruled
by such war-mongering groups?"

In August 1914 the war broke out. Many
Frenchmen, most of whom were not at all militaristically
inclined, were forced to join the army. I experienced
some sobering moments firsthand when the reserves at
one of the railway stations had to say goodbye to their
wives and children. It was heartbreaking. What was
there for me to do? When I returned to the plant the
next day, everybody was gone. So I went to the Swiss
Consul to see what was expected of me. A man standing
outside was handing out military notices. At that time
there were about thirty thousand Swiss in Paris, and
they were all instructed to go home as soon as possible.
Switzerland was not at war.

Every day we went to the station to see if there was a

train. There were none except for the reserves who were
being called up. We had to fend for ourselves.
Unfortunately we had to exchange our Swiss francs for
French francs. For 100 Swiss francs we got only 72
French francs. Since I had 150 francs, I lost a
considerable amount of money.

My transactions completed, I packed my luggage
and went again to the station. A freight train would be
leaving that noon for Melun, so we boarded a cattle car.
We left Paris very slowly and eventually arrived in
Dijon. There we were taken off the train and put into a
movie house, where we slept under guard. The next
morning another train took us to Pontarlier on the Swiss
border. At Pontarlier the railroad tracks had been torn
up, so we had to walk for two hours carrying our bags.
Eventually we found a farmer who agreed to let us use a
cart. Thus, our group of about 130 Swiss loaded our
luggage into the cart and took it to the Swiss border,
where we were well received by the Swiss army. The
next morning we continued our journey home.

Back home, I was drafted for military duty, and I
had to spend seven months in the military service,
without furlough, until 1915.

When I came home, Marie and I immediately
applied for a marriage license. During the first three
months of our marriage we lived in a two-room
apartment while I worked in a textile machine
department. We spent three beautiful months
together—heaven on earth, full of violins, full of
expectations. Then I received a summons to join the
army again within five days. This time I served seven
months without furlough and with very little
compensation. Mother had to go in search of food, and
we had to draw from my savings, but somehow we
survived.

In 1916 our son Carl Walter was born, and two years
later, toward the end of the war, Louis was born. Then
the flu epidemic broke out. I came down with an ear
infection and hovered for weeks between life and death.
I was grateful to my Father in heaven for his answer to

our prayers, for I finally became well, and I resolved to work in the Church more diligently than I had ever done before.

After completing my military service, I returned to my former job. Later I worked for a firm that made trucks for the German army. When the German army collapsed, the company had orders for 72 million Swiss francs [$15 million]. Germany couldn't take the trucks or pay for them, so the company went bankrupt, and we went on strike. I was active as cashier of the labor organization and had to deal with seventeen other men who collected dues. Because of the strike the labor leaders were discharged. As one of them, I was thrown out and blacklisted—I could not find work anywhere.

So what was there for me to do? Amazingly, by that time Marie and I had saved 2,000 Swiss francs. However, we had two children and another on the way. Brother Wilhelm Bartel was in touch with a German coal dealer who wanted to dispose of German war supplies. He offered me a carload of paper bags. I paid 2,000 francs for the bags and started selling in advance. Then the car arrived—and a customs bill was presented for 4,050 francs. Since I didn't have any more money, what was I to do? I had already taken orders for 20,000 bags. So the coal dealer said, "I will advance you the money." I guess he concluded that I looked honest, for he had no other reason for extending me credit in the amount of 4,000 francs. "I'm sure you will pay me as soon as you can," he said. The first thousand francs that I had, I took to him immediately.

I sold all the bags and then met a Mr. Custer, who managed a drugstore. He said, "I also import paper bags. How about your selling mine? I have too many." They were the right size for 50 kilograms of cement, which was being imported to Holland. I went to an exporter of cement with the suggestion that he buy my bags, and he gave me an order immediately. Fourteen days later I took Mr. Custer his money. Two months later he asked me if I wouldn't like to come and sell for him on a regular basis. I agreed, so I slowly liquidated all my paper bags and started to work for Mr. Custer.

At this point I would like to say something about tithing. It is a holy principle for me. I had a very precious experience at that time when we had reached rock bottom financially. Our income was inadequate for our family—we had three children. This was about the time I started to work for Mr. Custer. I started working for a commission; the first month I made 200 francs [$35]. The second month I made only 145 francs. Business was very slow. On fast Sunday when I arrived at Church I met Brother Carl Edward Hoffmann, a very precious man who told me of a rich experience that started for him in 1914.

Brother Hoffmann was an architect and wanted to go to America. To this end he had saved 13,000 German marks [about $3,000]. However, President Valentine of the Swiss-German Mission called him on a mission. Without questioning authority, he went on the mission in 1914, and was assigned to serve in his native Germany. During World War I Brother Hoffmann served in the German army medical corps. After six weeks' service a shell exploded in front of him and a comrade as they were bringing the wounded back from one of the trenches. The explosion killed his companion, and Brother Hoffman's leg was so severely wounded that it had to be amputated. The army doctors tried to console him by telling him how well he could get along with a crutch. "I don't want one," he said. "I am an architect, and what I want is an artificial limb that will permit me to earn my living." While he was still in the hospital, he was called as a mission leader in Germany by the Swiss-German Mission president in Basel, Switzerland.

So Brother Hoffmann directed the affairs of the mission in Germany from his bedside in the hospital during World War I. Every Sunday morning he brought the patients together around his bed and taught them the gospel. All told, he bore his testimony to about two hundred people. Toward the end of the war he was finally released.

After the war, like many others, he had no work, no place to live, and was still an invalid. In Switzerland he was just one of some 250 architects and designers who were out of work. He was permitted to eat at Brother Feh's and sleep at Brother Mussig's. During the day he walked the streets looking for work. Mornings and evenings he poured out his soul to the Lord in fervent prayer. He cried, "Father, I sacrificed to you everything I had—my savings, my leg, and my time. Today I have no work. Now it is up to you to help me."

Finally he found a job in an architectural firm. And soon he had a lot of work. In fact, he had so much work that one day his supervisor told him, "Mr. Hoffmann, we are very sorry, but you will now have to come to work on Sunday." Brother Hoffmann, who was serving as district president in the Church, replied, "I'll have to think about this." He fasted about it, then told his supervisor, "I'm sorry—on Sundays I have a different master." "Well, then," his boss said, "you will have to leave this job." Before he left the job, he was able to find a different position that was worth 300 francs more in salary per month. "All the credit for this blessing I give to the payment of tithing," he said. "I had to pay tithing on money that I had to have. But the Lord blessed me abundantly."

Before I heard his testimony that day I had told myself that I would not be able to tithe my salary. Now I decided that instead of 14 francs, I would donate 15 francs in tithing. Next month I earned more than twice as much, 290 francs. Within six months my income quadrupled to about 600 francs. That was just the amount I required to feed and clothe my growing family. But then heaven ceased to bless us with money—he gave me four times as many children. I think I also grew four times in wisdom during that time.

After a few years my boss said, "I am tired of my business—too much work for me. Why don't you take it over? See if you can find some money to buy into it." So I found two co-signers and was able to get credit from a bank for the amount required. This was the way I was able to go into business for myself. For six years I ran the business. Then in the early 1930s one customer after another was losing his money during the early stages of the depression and could not pay me. This forced me to decide whether or not to liquidate. I wrote my customers and asked them to pay, and wrote my creditors and asked them to be patient. One of my suppliers was a Mr. Fries, a wealthy businessman. One day he came to my office while I was away visiting my customers. He said to my wife, "I heard that you are going to liquidate. Why?" "We don't have any more money," she replied. "I have been thinking about a plan for some time," he told her. "I have to put money into my big business. How would it be if he were to travel for me? I have heard good things about him."

So I liquidated and started working for Mr. Fries. That was in 1932, the depths of the depression. I stayed with him for thirty-seven years. All my business dealings have left me with a good conscience. I never ever cheated any one of my customers. Among them I had the reputation of living a correct and honest life. Regrettably, not too many of my customers knew that I was a Mormon, for I was too rushed in my daily work to take much time talking religion.

From the beginning, as I traveled, I faced the temptation of drinking alcohol. Tobacco was no problem because I couldn't even stand to smell it. But what would I drink in restaurants? All they had was mineral water and soft drinks, which most Europeans considered too sweet. I visited many restaurants in which alcohol was the only beverage served. One day when I was visiting a customer, a restaurant owner, I was drinking raspberry juice and he asked, "Do you drink this crazy drink all day long? You'll get blue intestines." I answered, "Well, if you have another drink without alcohol that is profitable for you to sell, please let me have it." So he brought me some mineral water. Two months later I paid him a visit and found him sitting at the breakfast table. Beside him was a bottle of mineral water. I asked "What's the matter with you, Mr. Angst?

You'll get blue intestines." "My stomach won't let me drink wine any more. I have to stop."

This is the way I did missionary work. All I had to do was to be a Mormon. I didn't have to talk about it. With diligent study I began to learn more about the gospel and had singular experiences. I was made a Sunday School teacher, and in 1922 a counselor in the branch presidency. In 1924 I was ordained an elder when I was called to be a branch president.

With the passing of years my testimony has gained in depth. Since the age of six years I have never entertained any doubt about the truthfulness of the Church. I have studied and pondered all kinds of philosophies, but this has generally been a waste of time.

When I was about twenty-five years old I had an experience that illustrates the importance of the scriptures and the need for humility. In a priesthood meeting the class got off the subject of the lesson and started a fruitless discussion. One of the members couldn't put up with it any longer. I made a comment that angered him so much that he looked for a scripture. Then he arose, quoted the scripture, closed the Bible, sat down, and didn't say another word. It was like a slap on the hand, because it negated all that I had said.

I walked home with the branch president, and he said, "Today you were really set straight for once." I replied, "Yes, it bothers me greatly. I think I had better write that brother a letter." The branch president said, "Go ahead, but I think you should wait for eight days." After eight days I decided not to write the letter. I learned a lesson that I didn't forget throughout my life. From that day on I never again attempted to answer a question in a discussion based solely on my own opinion. This is why I always have the scriptures with me; I know the scriptures much better now, and I answer with them.

The branch grew until it was divided into two, for emigration to America did not play an important role in the 1920s. During the 1920s and the 1930s with the rise of the National Socialists [the Hitler movement] we had some problems in our branches. We also had

inexperienced leaders who didn't understand many of
the programs of the Church. And as World War II
began, nearly all communication with the States was cut
off. It was a difficult period for all of us. But we didn't let
the dissensions and disunity get us down. We made up
for our inexperience and problems with a great deal of
enthusiasm. I believe also those trials strengthened us,
and this is why I am persevering to the end.

During World War II Brother Max Zimmer became
the "caretaker president" for the Church in Basel. I had
been called in 1938 to be president of the Zurich
District, and until 1943 I worked very closely with
Brother Zimmer. Then one day I came home from work
and found an order to join the army. I served for six
months.

After I returned home I served in an elders quorum
presidency, then as a counselor in the mission presidency
under President Scott Taggart. When President Taggart
was released I was released also, but it wasn't long until I
was called to be in charge of the Sunday Schools of the
Swiss-Austrian Mission.

Two years before this call came, I had started taking
English lessons at an evening school. I didn't clearly
know why at the time. When President Samuel
Bringhurst called me to direct the Sunday School work,
he handed me an *Instructor* magazine, for we didn't have
any handbooks. He said, "Here is the *Instructor*. Will you
please see if you can organize the Sunday School here
like it is organized in America." Of course, I didn't know
what Sunday Schools were like in America. But I started
immediately and began translating the *Instructor*. Often I
would return home from a Sunday School visit at
midnight or one o'clock in the morning and would then
write and translate articles for our quarterly bulletin.
The bulletin sometimes contained forty pages of
translated articles for use by Sunday School teachers. I
also contacted all of the Sunday Schools to get
information on their status. Their responses indicated
that of twenty-three Sunday Schools, only one was being
conducted in full conformity with the instructions from

the general board—so I had a real challenge. I served in this position for ten years.

In 1959 I visited in America for the first time. While I was there President William S. Erekson was called as mission president to serve in Switzerland. He visited me there and when I returned home that fall he said, "I would like to release you from your position as Sunday School superintendent and to call you to serve once more as district president in Zurich." And so I returned to the position that I had held early in the war years. Later I was called to serve as stake patriarch, a position that has blessed me immeasurably.

A long lifetime of experiences in my life has merged into a strong testimony and conviction. When I have made mistakes, I have had to pay for them, and I have asked for forgiveness. I have been in situations among men many times when I had to stand alone, with no earthly help or solace. I have had to overcome seemingly insurmountable obstacles. But the Lord has blessed me as I have grown in knowledge and experience, and it is the sum of these experiences that has given me an unwavering testimony. I especially treasure the precious messages of the General Authorities. If I were to disclose what experiences have strengthened my testimony the most, I would put the listening and reading of these addresses at the very top. Some important details of doctrine have become clear to my mind only through lengthy and prayerful reflection. I know that God lives and that Joseph Smith was called by him to restore the Church.

(*Note: Karl Ringger died of cancer in Zurich on March 25, 1974, one month before his eighty-fourth birthday. His beloved Maria died June 7, 1975, at age eighty-five. Both were buried in Zurich.*)

11

CARL AND LOUIS RINGGER: THE SECOND GENERATION

Our grandmother had one child, our father. When he was two years old his father died and was buried in Zurich, but we don't know where. In Switzerland, because there is so little land available, people are buried in pine boxes paid for by the city, and after thirty years the graves are leveled and the land used all over again. Consequently, the graves of our brothers and sisters who died early are already gone, and in a few years our grandmother's grave will be destroyed.

When we were young, we held family home evenings. Elder Thomas E. McKay was president of the European Mission during 1922-24, and he started family night throughout all the European missions. We had regular family nights every Wednesday night until 1939, or the beginning of World War II.

Our father learned to speak foreign languages on his own, including Swiss, German, French, English, and Italian. As patriarch, he gave blessings in German, and they were then translated. When the Swiss Temple was dedicated, there weren't any other patriarchs in Europe, so many people, when they came to visit the temple, also

came to Father for blessings. There are now LDS
families of many nationalities and languages, all the way
from Finland to the Pacific islands, who have received
blessings under his hands.

As a family, economically and financially we had a
really rough time. We never had much as far as worldly
possessions are concerned, but we always had enough to
eat, and Dad was never out of work, which he attributed
to paying his tithing. Though he had no previous
training in music, for twenty years he directed the
branch choir. He taught us to sing at home, at family
home evening. We had a family choir of our own, and
also learned to play the piano.

In Zurich, as in many branches in the mission field,
each member had to hold two or three or even more
positions. During the time Father was directing the choir
he was an MIA teacher, MIA president, Sunday School
teacher, and member of the branch presidency. He later
served as branch president, then district president, and
assistant to the mission president. He used to take his
children by turns to visit the branches, so we had the
experience of seeing him fulfill his callings.

Our own branch was prosperous and active at first.
Then people started to find fault with one another, and
attendance declined greatly. Finally, in the 1950s, the
missionaries began to have some success in Switzerland.
The Zurich Branch gained new life, and when the Swiss
Stake was organized in the summer of 1961, the branch
was divided into two wards. The temple has brought
great spiritual benefits to the members there.

Another problem that led to the decline in
membership was that many strong LDS families
emigrated to America, particularly some of the strongest
leaders. That's the way it was until the construction of
the temple, which gave the Church there a whole new
outlook.

Louis remembers his own decision to leave
Switzerland and emigrate to America: "Economically I
had no reason to leave. I had a good job, a responsible
position with a good employer. But my wife's parents

had moved to Salt Lake City, and she felt that we should take our family and go there also, primarily because she wanted to be married in the temple. It took me one year to make that decision, and I think I never would have come here if there had been a temple in Europe at that time. The spirit of gathering was really a desire to have the blessings of the temple."

One of the problems in missionary work in Switzerland has been that the people are basically happy with what they have and resent change. For this reason, the mission tends toward a low yield of converts.

As boys, we were interested in scouting, but we had no success in having a scout troop in our branch. In Switzerland each troop has to be chartered with the Swiss scouting organization, and must be directed by a scoutmaster who has a diploma from that organization based on passing certain tests. Finally in our town a nondenominational scouting unit was organized. We joined this group, and this was our thrilling experience. Louis became the first Mormon boy who received the Swiss Fieldmaster diploma. In Switzerland there aren't old men directing troops—Fieldmasters are young men of eighteen or so. And for that reason Louis is still in scouting today.

Because of the regulations governing scout organizations, in Switzerland (and most European countries) it is difficult to have the scout program as part of the Church's youth program. The connections between the Church and scouting that are found in the United States do not exist in Europe. The way to build a scout unit is to build a tradition, and it is difficult to have a good troop until that tradition is built. Our father had the foresight to see what was needed in our branch; he brought into the scouting organization outside help. The troop was sponsored by a group of parents in the city, with boys from all religions.

The significant difference between American troops and those in Switzerland is that in America there is a handbook for everything, and it is easy to train leaders and boys. In Switzerland, there is only one manual. We had to write our own manuals for patrol leaders and troop leaders. There isn't a trained professional staff, either; the Swiss Fieldmaster does the job only part-time.

When we were boys in the 1930s, most of the people we worked with were members of the Social Democratic political party, and they thought scouting should be used for physical fitness and to teach boys love of country, which meant love of the army. Many people compared the Swiss scouts with the Hitler movement in Germany.

In those days the Church didn't have a good image in Switzerland. Members of the established churches looked down on Mormons as a sect or cult or strange religious group. Even today the Church is not legally accepted as a church in Switzerland. Only the Catholic Church, the Reformed Church, the Protestant Church (including the Zwinglis and Lutherans), the Calvin Church, and the Jews are recognized.

Also in those early years, most of the members were very poor, and there were few professional people. In all of Switzerland we had only one member who had a college education: Wilhelm Zimmer, an architect who was in charge of building the Swiss Temple. Louis was the second Latter-day Saint in Switzerland to receive formal advanced education.

In Switzerland young men on our income level who were called into the Swiss army never had opportunities to become officers. Later this restriction eased a bit and our brother Hans became a colonel. But social traditions did not allow upward mobility for people who started low on the ladder. Church members suffered under this problem.

In the old days the average member walked to services, rain or shine. We walked about two miles in the morning to priesthood meeting and Sunday School, and then we walked two miles back home. In the evening we again walked two miles to go to sacrament meeting at seven o'clock. On Sunday afternoons whole families went for walks in nearby forests, as was the custom in Europe. Some families had to walk even farther to church. There were some streetcars, but not many could afford to pay the fare four times a day, so attendance at meetings fluctuated depending on the available money.

Usually Father studied the scriptures on Sunday afternoons. He was a good speaker, and he never used notes for his talks. One of his favorite sayings was, "The Lord takes nothing out of an empty barrel," meaning an empty mind.

In our high school of about two thousand students, there were only two Latter-day Saints. In the secondary grades, students are taught the religion of the Reformed Church, and Catholics go to their own special classes one or two hours a week. Louis signed up for a class taught by a former Reformed Church minister, and they had most exciting conversations. Louis was a deacon then. Years later that same minister was the regimental chaplain in Louis's infantry regiment. Once during World War II he talked about the resurrection in a church service. It was obvious to Louis that he didn't believe in the resurrection, so afterward Louis approached him and discussed the subject with him and a circle of other officers and soldiers.

The Church had a reputation of being an American church, so people didn't accept it because it was foreign. It is still considered an American religion, especially in France, which hurts the work because so many Europeans are not pro-American. And since most Swiss now have good incomes, they are satisfied with their lives and not quick to make changes.

Through all those years of growing up, we had the missionaries in our home once a week, on Tuesday afternoons, for dinner. As we look back, we can see that our father had an open mind. He wanted to find out about things, and the missionaries were a source of great information. In the mission field we looked upon the nineteen-year-old Mormon missionary as the representative of the prophet, and we respected and treated him as such. The Church was our father's life. Earning a living was necessary to feed his family, but every spare moment, all his interests were within the framework of the Church. That's what made him a great teacher and a great man.

Father often had lengthy discussions with his customers. They knew about his religious affiliation. He was very successful, and they loved him dearly. We have never seen personal relationships develop in our work here in America that compare with those that developed between our dad and his customers. When Louis went back to Zurich on a trip one year, he took Father and Mother on a drive and stopped to see some of these old customers. There was still real warmth and deep interhuman feelings expressed that had been established so many years before.

III
UNTO THE LATIN AMERICANS

12

RESOUNDING FAITH IN GUATEMALA

Latin America includes most of the continental western hemisphere—Mexico, Central America, and South America. The majority of Latin Americans speak Spanish or Portugese and live in the cities. They are the "Ladinos," or non-Indians, and it is primarily among these people that the Church has directed its work and has met with such extraordinary success.

But there is a sizeable population in Mexico, Central America, and South America that is strictly Indian—full-blooded and full-cultured. Often these people know no Spanish or Portuguese, no language but their own local tongues, which they inherited from their fathers and which can be traced back through history to aboriginal Incas, Mayas, and Aztecs, or any of a number of other groups. There are about twenty million Indians living in Latin America, and among most of them, Mormon missionary work has just begun.

Latin American Indians typically live in areas outside the cities in villages, hamlets, and small towns. They visit the cities only for the weekly market, to sell their wares and to purchase their daily needs to barter. Ac-

cording to Robert Blair of the BYU faculty, who is the
foremost LDS authority on the languages of Indian
Latin America, "The so-called cities of the ancient
Mayans were not cities as we now perceive them. They
were not centers of population, but religious centers. The
people did not live in those great Mayan structures, the
pyramids, but lived as they do today, making pil-
grimages to these centers from nearby and far away. The
Aztecs and the Incas may have had city life more as we
know it, but the Mayans did not enjoy that blessing."

For the most part, the Latin American Indians have
been rural peoples for more than two thousand years.
Although their towns are politically and economically
dominated by the Latins, in many areas the Indians out-
number the Spanish-speaking people by a large margin.
And they represent a special kind of challenge and opportunity for the expanding Church.

Situated in Central America between Mexico and El
Salvador is Guatemala, a country of diversity and
contrast, both in geography and people, and one that
well illustrates this point. The total population of the
country was about six million in 1978, more than half of
whom are Mayan Indians. The rest are mainly people of
Spanish descent. The distribution of Indians and
Ladinos varies greatly from one region to another.
However, Indians constitute at least two-thirds of the
population in the western highlands and the north
central areas, and over ninety percent are Indians in
Alta Verapaz, Solola, and Totonicapan. In general, Indians have not only survived the Spanish Conquest in
Guatemala but have also continued to remain the pre-
dominant element in the population of the country. Although a certain amount of race mixture and accultura-
tion has taken place between Indians and whites, this
has not been sufficient to obliterate their ethnic and
cultural identity, nor even to reduce them to a numerical
minority.

One of the languages of the Mayan family is
Cakchiquel, spoken by Indians living in many small
villages of western Guatemala. There are about 400,000

Cakchiquel Indians in Guatemala, most of whom are farmers; a few own their own small plots of land, but the majority rent land from the large plantation owners.

Patzicia is a Cakchiquel village of approximately ten thousand people. The village has one school, a small medical clinic operated by the government, and a Mormon chapel that has been the most striking and most beautiful building in the area. In this farming area, the main products of the people are corn, beans, rope, woven materials, and leather goods. There are about 325 Cakchiquel Latter-day Saints in this village.

In the context of the command that the restored gospel must be taken to all kindreds and tongues, Patzicia is a rather unusual outpost of the Church. Mormons there are very conscious of kinship ties: one's kindred is one's family, and kinship units are, of course, the basic foundation of the Church. In times past the spread of the gospel has not characteristically been an effort of families teaching their own kindred, or of teaching the message by means of one's own living blood relatives. Yet this has been the pattern in Patzicia, and in large part, it explains the growth of the Church in that village. The success of the proselyting effort among the Patzicia Indians is an example of how the gospel can be spread primarily through kinship ties. The Church has grown among the Cakchiquels primarily from family to family, rather than from missionary to individual converts.

The conversion of a native Indian, Daniel Mich, in the late 1950s led to the conversion of his extended family: brothers and sisters, uncles and aunts, sons and daughters. The Mich family was the beginning of an expanding Church community. Following this established nucleus, other kindred groups have developed within the local branch. The Church has been built not by "one of a city or two of a family," but to a surprising degree it has been built upon the recognition and use of native kindred ties.

Pablo Choc, whose personal story follows in these pages, lives in Patzicia. He is the father of a first-generation Cakchiquel Mormon family with long-standing roots there. They are hardworking and industrious people. They till the soil and do it well, despite their primitive tools.

Income studies of the Guatemalan Indians by Boyce Lines, a Mormon agricultural missionary, provide interesting figures on economic conditions in the Patzicia area. The median earning power of a typical family in 1977 was less than two hundred U.S. dollars a year. There is little cash flow. It is subsistence living. Farmers eat their own produce and barter it.

The Choc family are fairly typical of local Church members in income and life-style. They speak Cakchiquel at home, though Pablo has learned Spanish for convenience in meeting the outside world. He speaks fluent but not high Spanish, not a Spanish that has enabled him to understand Spanish literature. Therefore, in some respects the Book of Mormon is to him still a closed book, though after years of study and practice, he feels close to understanding its meaning. His sons are better prepared because they have attended school.

Pablo Choc's conversion to the Church has resulted in the conversion of his own family, his in-laws, and other immediate friends. His own recorded story affirms the capacity of the Church to reach the rural peoples, including the largely uneducated, and widely scattered Indians of Latin America.

Pablo Choc's second son, Daniel, was the first Mormon of Cakchiquel ancestry to serve as a fulltime missionary among his people in Guatemala. Prior to his mission call in 1975, he had received only two years of formal education. He had received no previous scholastic training, no drill or memorization work, and very little theological study.

Daniel Choc was reared among farmers in the village of Patzicia and its neighboring fields. He did not own a pair of shoes until he was sixteen years of age. His was a simple, uncomplicated life. But according to his missionary companions, he was never ashamed of his Indian heritage; he never wished to become a Ladino.

Julio Salazar, one of Daniel's companions, himself a native of Guatemala, detected within Daniel a struggle between being an Indian and being a Lamanite. He observed that Daniel "seemed always to have a great desire to know what it meant to be a Lamanite and to understand himself through understanding the people of the Book of Mormon. He seemed particularly impressed with the message of the seventeenth chapter of 4 Nephi, that after the visit of Christ there were no more Lamanites or any 'ites,' but that 'they were in one, the children of Christ, and heirs to the kingdom of God.' He seemed always to wish that we could understand the meaning of that principle.

"Elder Choc was a very humble person. Those Indians who gain education usually become proud and join the Ladinos. Some even change their names. If their Indian name is Cumes, they change it to Gomes, a Ladino name. But Daniel didn't like that. He didn't approve of such compromises. I admired him for this. As a missionary he was given new opportunities to associate with higher class people, but this didn't seem to change him at all."

Daniel himself has said that "the most important single thing that I have learned since I joined the Church is the meaning of the law of chastity," and this deserves special comment. Among Daniel's people, marriage is not traditionally important. Usually a local man will find a young woman and begin living with her. Later they may feel the necessity of a formal ceremony, but they are usually faithful to each other as husband and wife even though they may not be legally married. Daniel is no doubt suggesting here that young people in his home country do not understand chastity and the sanctity of marriage––or of marriage as a basic element in a "new and everlasting covenant"––as perceived by members of the Church. But the gospel changed Daniel's view of himself and of life as part of an eternal destiny.

According to his mission president and his missionary companions, Daniel was not only absolutely clean and pure in his thoughts, but also exceptionally eager to teach the gospel to his people and to improve himself. In tracting, he rarely walked, but would trot from gate to gate in his enthusiasm to share the gospel message.

One of his friends suggested that Daniel "was a shovel, not a hoe." With the hoe, Guatemalans are always pulling things toward themselves; with the shovel they are pushing things out, in a forward motion. Daniel moved forward away from himself, always seemingly full of concern and compassion. He was close and confidential with his father; he continually expressed love for his family and was always anxious for their welfare.

Until he became a converted Latter-day Saint, Daniel Choc continued to do things as they have always been done by his people. The restored gospel elevated his thoughts and gave him new appreciations, new opportunities, and new ideas. This is the overriding theme of the comments that follow, which he made in a brief interview conducted in a humble missionary apartment in Guatemala in June 1975.

In the pages that follow are the stories of Pablo Choc and his son Daniel.

13

PABLO CHOC'S STORY

I, Pablo Choc Loch, was born in Patzicia, Guatemala. My father was Antonio Choc Yancoba and my mother was Tomasa Loch Bac. I am the last of seven brothers. My family has always been very poor. We have worked in agriculture, tending the fields. For some seasons my father worked in business, buying goods in Guatemala City and bringing them to the village to sell. He also bought and sold merchandise on the coast in the country. He used to walk some fifty miles carrying the merchandise on his back to go from Patzicia to the coast. It was very hard work, but he made more money that way than staying in Patzicia and cultivating the land. With the little extra money he made, he bought us clothing and other needful things for the home.

Only my brother Francisco and I had an opportunity to attend school. It was not really intended by my parents that we should attend school, but there was a law in the land that all children eight years and older should attend school.

The officers found us tending our animals one day and they simply took us to school, and our parents had to go along with the idea. I am grateful that happened, for I learned many things in school, and had some very pleasant experiences there, but there were some hard times also.

My school years were suddenly ended by a revolution in our town, and many Latins and Indians were killed. A great antagonism and prejudice toward Indians was begun so we were not allowed to attend school anywhere. That was 1944, a year of much political turmoil.

One afternoon a plane flew by our village throwing out a lot of handbills urging the people to go to the main square. Indians and Latins gathered there, mostly out of curiosity. Over the loudspeakers we were told that the previous government had been overthrown and a military politburo now held the reigns of power. The previous government had been very paternalistic toward the Indian people and had granted them many benefits. Now that it had been overthrown, the Latins felt they could do anything they wanted with the Indians again. So right there in the main square some Latins began to abuse some Indians and a big fight was started. Some who had brought their guns with them killed fourteen Indians and injured many more. When their ammunition was used up they hid in the house of one of the richest men in the town.

The Indians were furious. They gathered and broke into that house and killed many of the Latins inside. Then the Latins sent for help to the neighboring towns. Soldiers were quickly sent to put down the revolt, and they killed great numbers of Indians that evening. With the help of the soldiers, they broke into the homes of many Indians, killed them, and dragged them out bodily. I was eleven years old at the time. I remember vividly how some of the injured and killed of my people were dragged from their houses and were left lying on the streets for three or more days, and how dogs and scavengers came to eat the bodies.

After this a great bitterness took over in the Indians' relationships with the Latins. We didn't work for them

any more as we used to, and we put forth even greater
efforts to be completely self-sufficient.

Many of the Indians who participated in the revolt
were taken to prison in Guatemala City. Some stayed
there for as long as eight years. They suffered greatly,
but this also brought great progress to our people,
because while they were there, they were taught manual
and industrial skills. They were also taught to read and
write. When they returned, many set up carpenter shops,
mechanical shops, and tailor shops. Others were also
trained as masons, plumbers, and construction workers.
Because of this, a few years later some of the families
were able to buy some land and a few animals. Thus,
much progress resulted from that tragic revolution.

When I was fifteen my father bought some horses,
and from that time on I began to accompany him on his
trips to the coast and to the cities to buy and sell
merchandise. We did this during the summers; the rest
of the year we stayed home to cultivate our lands.

When I was eighteen, I decided to get married to
Augustina, a girl I had known for about a year. My
parents were very old and I knew that soon they would
pass away, and I did not want to be left by myself in the
house. My brother Francisco also decided to get married
that year.

So with the consent of our parents we decided to
have a double wedding. I thought this would be a lot of
fun and it would also save us some money, for we would
have only one wedding reception. In line with Catholic
tradition we each asked two friends to go with us to the
municipality records office to serve as witnesses. We were
married by the civil law; then we went to the Catholic
cathedral to be married by the priest according to the
church's law. That ceremony cost five dollars apiece.
This would be the equivalent of more than a month's
wages. But because we were brothers and being married
at the same time, the Catholic priest charged us nine
quetzales [equivalent to nine dollars]. After that
ceremony we went to our home and had a very nice
party. We had a marimba, lots of food, and lots to drink.

Such receptions are very expensive. The parents help a
little, but my brother and I had to work very hard to
save the money to pay the expenses. Afterwards, because
my parents were very old, they asked us to stay with
them. So my wife helped my mother, and I continued to
help my father in the fields, and we stayed with them for
a whole year because they did not want us to leave.
Then I decided to build my own home.

Two children were born to us, and then we had the
very difficult experience of the death of our third child.
As the children were growing, I needed to make more
money, so I began to travel to the coast to sell
merchandise to the farmers there. This is quite a
common custom among our people, especially during
the summers when there is not much work to be done on
our farms. The women and the children stay behind and
the men go to the coast to work on the big plantations
for two or three months. With the extra money I earned
during those months I bought clothes for the children
and other necessities for our home.

Our house was a very simple one consisting of only
one big room, with a couple of beds and a few chairs. We
cooked on an open fire inside the house, and some of us
had to sleep on the floor. This was the situation with
most families in our village. We also suffered from
plagues of lice and fleas and other bugs. These plagues
became so unbearable that the government had to send
men to fumigate our homes and our animals. Many
people were afraid of being poisoned by the insecticide,
but after they had fumigated our homes we slept so
comfortably that everybody was convinced of the
goodness of it. We were truly grateful to the government
for its help.

Little by little we were progressing. The wages of
common laborers were increased to fifty cents a day. I
remember when I was eight years old it was only eight
cents per day, and now, in 1975, it is over eighty cents.
Another thing that helped us in those years was the
introduction of chemical fertilizer. Again, some people
were afraid to try this innovation because they were

afraid it might poison their food. But as they saw how
rapidly and abundantly the crops grew, they were
converted to the idea. Chemical fertilizer also made it
possible to plant things during the summer. With the
extra money we earned through improved crops we were
able to buy more land and improve our condition
generally, so that we no longer had to go to the coasts
and work almost like slaves in the big plantations.

Another progressive move came when they began
building the Pan American highway, which passes right
through our village. Many of our people were employed
as highway workers. I worked for about twenty days and
earned twenty-five dollars. This was a lot of money at
that time when we were making only fifty cents a day.
Although we were making more money, our condition
remained pretty much the same because the prices of
goods went up also.

Now let me tell you about my religious struggle. I
was raised in a Catholic home, but I seldom went to
church. As a child I was taught the different prayers of
the Catholic faith and I still remember a few of them.
When I was fifteen or sixteen I stopped going to church
completely. A few years later some friends invited me to
attend the Bethel Church. This was an evangelical
church, and they motivated me to read the New
Testament for the first time. During those years there
was a strong trend to join the Bethel Church in our
village. However, as I attended their meetings I was
somewhat disappointed by their inconsistencies, and
some friends also pointed out to me the different ways in
which they had departed from the original teachings of
the Lord. The same feelings came over me when I went
to the Catholic Church so I decided to remain aloof; I
attended Catholic mass only during festivals or special
celebrations.

As the years passed, I became totally disillusioned
with the Catholic Church. I knew in my heart that the
truth was not there. I continued reading the New
Testament, though, and I continued to inquire from
people who belonged to other religious sects as to the

beliefs of their churches. I was disillusioned with all of
them, but I continued to search.

Sixteen years ago, I had my first glimpse of The
Church of Jesus Christ of Latter-day Saints. At that time
I was struggling within myself to decide whether I would
believe in the Christian God or in the pagan idols that
our people worshiped. My wife had been raised in a
home of devout idol worshipers, and whenever an illness
came over a member of our family, she would insist that
I go to the Brujo, the shaman, and get a
recommendation from him as to what idol I should go
to, to offer up my sacrifices. There was a time when our
firstborn was very ill. I took him to the shaman, and
after his ceremonial prayers he advised me to go to the
Judas idol and offer up sacrifices there, which I did.
Amazingly, the child was healed for a time. He did not
completely recover, however, and soon after that he
began to get worse. My wife insisted that I take him
back to the shaman, and he recommended that I go and
offer up sacrifices to the Judas idol again. When I got
there, many people were burning incense and offering
up prayers and sacrifices before the wooden idol. After
everybody had left I went up by the idol and asked
myself in all earnestness, "Is this my god? Do I believe in
him?" Suddenly I realized that I did not believe in that
idol, that I knew that somewhere out there in the silence
was my Heavenly Father, my God.

I had heard that if you go up to an idol without faith
there will be a commotion in the room, and while I
completely despised myself for being in the presence of
the wooden image, I did hear noises as though the image
was shaking. I left, and I have never returned to it again.

It was at that time that I was first introduced to the
Latter-day Saint church. My neighbor and good friend
Daniel Mich, who was a Mormon, invited me to attend
funeral services that were being conducted in his home
for his mother, who had passed away. The missionaries
conducted the meeting, and there was a very peaceful
feeling. They sang hymns whose words touched my
heart deeply, and they offered prayers that were very

meaningful. At that moment I knew that one day I
would join that church, for I felt a familiar spirit in their
teachings. I went home hoping that some day those
missionaries would come and visit me.

The missionaries were an inspiration to me. They
dressed with great dignity and were always respectful
and courteous. They met great opposition. At one time a
group of Catholics got together to throw them out of
town. Using sticks and stones and machetes, they took
the missionaries to the mayor of the city to be judged for
charges of deception and blasphemy. But they were
protected and allowed to continue their labors.

One day while I was working in the fields, they came
to our house. They asked for my brother Francisco, but
he was not interested at all and he did not invite them
in. When I came home that evening my children
informed me that the missionaries had been there, and I
felt very sad that I had missed them. I instructed my
children that if they should come back again, to please
ask them to return Saturday afternoon. To my joy they
did come back. Saturday afternoon I was somewhat
nervous when they knocked on my door. I opened it and
there they stood, dignified and clean, with subdued
expressions on their faces. They took off their hats
respectfully and introduced themselves as missionaries of
The Church of Jesus Christ of Latter-day Saints. I
explained to them that my house was very simple and I
had no place for them to sit down to share their message
with us. They assured me that that did not matter; they
would be happy to come in and explain the gospel to
me. So I invited them in.

They offered prayer, and during the prayer as they
asked Heavenly Father to bless my family, I sensed the
great love that they had for us as a people. My heart was
touched again, and I knew that they were true
representatives of Jesus Christ. And so they came back
again and again, and we always received them with
great joy. My wife did not come to the discussions but
my children did.

Soon the missionaries asked us to attend church with

them. I was embarrassed to go with them because I knew
I would face a lot of scorn from my neighbors and
relatives. They were already criticizing me for allowing
the elders to come to my home. So for the first few times
I did not accept their invitation to go to church, but one
day I did feel the desire to go. I did not want to go
myself, so I walked up the road where I knew Brother
Mich would pass by on his way to church. I met him
and asked if he would mind if I accompanied him to the
chapel. He said he would be delighted. We walked to the
chapel together and there I met the missionaries, who
were very glad to see me attending church. I felt great
peace during the services, and from that time on I have
never missed any meetings unless I was seriously ill. In
fact, so much did I enjoy the meetings that all week long
I looked forward to Sunday. To me it would be
wonderful if we could have meetings every night or if all
days were Sundays. I would get up very early Sunday
morning and be in the chapel before the rest of the
members arrived. There was a special spirit in the simple
building.

One day the missionaries asked me if I wanted to be
baptized. I said I would, but not yet. I was battling
within myself to leave the things of the world. I used to
drink a little bit and I enjoyed Catholic parties and
festivals. I realized that baptism was a serious covenant,
and I wanted to have a true conviction within my heart
that I was going to be able to forsake my sins and the
traditions of my parents forever. My wife was not very
happy with my intentions of becoming a member of The
Church of Jesus Christ of Latter-day Saints. She said
that it would be all right, but that she would not join
with me.

The day soon came when I felt impressed to commit
myself to baptism. When I told the missionaries, they
were very glad, and we set a date. During the
intervening days I fasted and prayed in earnest to
receive the strength to leave the past behind and enter
into the covenant of baptism. My son Serapio and my
nephew Carlos were baptized with me. It was a very

special meeting. Then the missionaries asked me to
attend priesthood meeting. As the months passed I was
ordained a deacon, a teacher, a priest, and finally an
elder.

Many responsibilities and opportunities to serve
came to my life in the Church. The Church purchased a
piece of land in Patzicia and we began to build a chapel.
My family and I worked faithfully to help build the
house of the Lord. My wife was becoming more and
more interested in the Church, but she still refused to
attend with us.

A little boy was born to us and my wife wanted him
baptized in the Catholic Church. But I knew better. I
knew that the Catholic Church was false and that the
gospel of Jesus Christ was true. So my wife and I had a
very difficult time making the decision. Finally I asked
the missionaries to come to my home to bless my child,
and I prepared some refreshments and invited our
family and neighbors so we could have a little ceremony
resembling some of our own traditions and yet comply
with the gospel of Jesus Christ. My wife was happy with
the atmosphere of that occasion and by the love and
concern of the missionaries. Our relationship was not
only saved, but it actually improved.

When the chapel was finished, the construction
supervisor asked me if I would serve as the custodian. He
said that since I had helped with the construction from
the very beginning, I would know how to repair things
that went wrong and how to take care of the different
installations. I did not want to accept, for I knew that I
would be separated from my family. I felt a great
responsibility to be with them, especially because my
wife was not converted yet. I also felt that other
members of the branch who were poorer than I should
receive the benefit of that salary. But he insisted that I
was better prepared for the job, and I have been
functioning as the custodian of our chapel ever since.

After Brother Fidel Cujcuj finished his term as
branch president I was called to that position. I have
worked hard because I am so new at such big

responsibilities. Often I have gone without breakfast and
lunch and come home late, tired and hungry, and my
wife has prepared me something to eat. Then I have
been able to tell her of wonderful things that happened
that day. My heart has been full of joy and satisfaction. I
have been a better man than I was, and my wife has felt
that, and she has become more and more appreciative of
the gospel.

I have received much persecution because of the
gospel, and there have been many temptations that have
been hard to overcome. However, my appreciation and
love for my family has increased also. I began to explain
the gospel to my wife with great love, and one day she
accepted the gospel and decided to be baptized. It was a
joyous occasion.

Now my whole family was active in the Church, and
we had no more arguments or conflicts in the home as
we had before we became members of the Church.
Instead we enjoyed great peace and satisfaction. Then
came to us the opportunity to go to the temple of the
Lord to be sealed for all eternity. We had to sacrifice
many things in order to go, and the mission president
also helped us considerably, but the sacrifice was worth
the joy that has come as a result of that sacred ordinance
in the Arizona Temple at Mesa.

One of my experiences in the Church that I have
enjoyed greatly is missionary work. For two years I
worked with the full-time missionaries as a local
missionary, and I learned much from those young men.
They were true disciples of the Lord Jesus Christ, and
they had to endure much tribulation. At one time
because of political unrest in town it was decreed that all
people should be in their homes by nine o'clock at night.
We were giving a gospel presentation at the home of an
investigator and it was past nine. Unknowingly, the
missionaries walked home. They were apprehended and
sent to prison that night, and the next morning they
were treated very harshly. But finally they were released.
People insulted them in the streets and threw stones at
them, but they were very humble and long-suffering, a

great example to the people of the town.

I remember when Brother Mich's mother died and the missionaries carried the coffin to the grave. Many of the Latins in town were astonished. They said among themselves, "How is it that North Americans are carrying an Indian on their shoulders?" Because of this great show of love toward the Indian people, many have accepted the gospel.

So this is the story of my life in the Church. It hasn't been an easy road. From the very beginning I met much opposition, both from neighbors and in my own home. Little by little we have grown in the gospel and become a happier family. My children have progressed greatly; my son Daniel is now serving as a full-time missionary. But it has been hard for us economically. Daniel saved a little money before he went and I helped him with some money to get started. I have also committed to help him with one hundred dollars a year. I wish I could support him with more, but I have ten children and many responsibilities, so it is impossible for me to do so. But he is doing a great job as a missionary. My other children are also progressing.

Perhaps the greatest problem that we have had in our family, and the problem that is most common to our people in Patzicia, is poverty. Because of it, we have much malnutrition and illiteracy. As a result of our poverty and ignorance we are treated disrespectfully by our brothers, the Latins. They consider us as if we were the dross of the earth. When we go to the government offices for whatever purposes, we are asked to wait outside. Often it takes two or three days for a simple birth certificate to be issued to us, while if other Latins come in for the same document they are attended to immediately. Slowly things are changing.

The mayor of our town now is an Indian, and that is making our burden a little lighter. As more Indians are becoming educated and improving their economic situation, we are becoming more accepted in the Latin community. We don't feel as different from them as we used to. In fact, a new generation is rising. Since they

don't know the atrocities committed against the Indian
people during 1944 revolution, they are friendly toward
the Latins, and the great gulf of hatred that separates us
is being bridged. Even those who were children at the
time of the massacre are forgetting somewhat. Recently
we held a town meeting in our chapel and invited the
mayor and other officers. Many Latins attended, and we
discussed the problem of drinkable water in our
community. There was a trusting and cooperative spirit
on the part of both Indians and Latins.

When the missionaries organized an open house,
several displays were set up and many of us participated.
The Catholic priest, the mayor of the city, other
important officials, and land owners were invited. One
night we had an attendance of about three hundred.
Even the Catholic priest, who we thought would not
come, visited one morning when there were only a few
people in attendance. I suppose he was a little
embarrassed to be seen by his members at the Mormon
chapel. But he expressed his admiration for some of the
programs of the Church, especially the recreational
program. He expressed great confidence in the future of
the Church, saying that many people from other
churches would join it. He praised our building as well.

I feel that in the near future we will see great
progress in the Church here in Patzicia. The seeds are
being sown abundantly and we will see the fruits soon. I
bear my testimony that I know this is the true Church of
Jesus Christ. From the time I was baptized on April 30,
1960, to this day, I have never doubted the truthfulness
of the gospel of Jesus Christ. Our lives have changed
considerably. We have had peace and happiness in our
family and great progress--even economic progress, for
we have been able to buy some land and animals and to
improve the conditions of our houses, our eating habits,
our personal cleanliness, and our education. The gospel
has been a great light in our lives, and we hope to enjoy
more and more of that divine light. We have suffered
much tribulation and have seen many of the members
and missionaries suffer physical abuse because of the

gospel. We recognize that Jesus Christ had to suffer much to save us all, and so the Saints must be proved also, and must endure persecution. I testify that this is a church of order and enlightenment. We have learned many things, especially how to organize ourselves and how to proceed in an orderly manner in the affairs of life. I remember vividly how well planned my baptism was. I was interviewed by the branch president and then by the district president, and the missionaries instructed me in all matters concerning my baptism. It was not taken lightly. It was a sacred ordinance, and all present felt that way.

I know that if we are faithful to the gospel of Jesus Christ we shall live with him and with our families in eternal happiness in the celestial kingdom of God.

14

DANIEL CHOC:
THE SECOND
GENERATION

The Mormon missionaries first came to our house
when I was about seven or eight years old. But I don't
have many impressions or memories of my childhood
days in the Church because I didn't attend meetings
very often. We had animals I had to take care of, even
on Sundays. But by age ten, I attended church more
often. I didn't have any friends to go to church with, so
that made it difficult for me. My friends were all
nonmembers, so they always tried to get me to play with
them on Sundays. They would say "Oh, don't go to
church." My father always tried to make me attend, and
when I didn't go he would be upset. He would come
home and lecture me, so often I hid from him.

As youngsters we noticed the North American
missionaries, and we often talked about them while
taking care of our animals. We had a lot of time in the
fields to talk about what we wanted to be or do in life.
Some would mention that they wanted to buy new
clothes, to dress better, or to buy other material things.
But I would tell them that I would like to learn to drive
a tractor or a car; I wanted to progress in many ways. I

can say that I had a strong desire to make something of myself even from a very young age.

When I was about twelve years old I began to work with my father in the fields. As I became a more effective worker I began to feel that I deserved to have better clothes and a better physical condition. However, my father was very poor, and I had many brothers and sisters, so I did not dare ask him to buy me the things I wanted so much. But my clothes were very old and poor looking, and as I reached fifteen, a time when most of the youth in our village begin to hope for more attractive clothes, I became impatient with my father, for he would not buy me anything new, although I worked with him very hard every day.

By this time some of my friends had gone away to Guatemala City to work and had earned enough money to buy fancy clothes and other things. They wanted me to go with them, but I did not want to accept their invitations because I knew my father would not approve. Besides, I knew that the youth who go to the capital city are tempted to do bad things. Some never return to the village again.

During this time my father became the president of the Patzicia Branch. He received communication from Cordell Andersen* that he wanted to recruit Mormon youngsters who were interested in learning improved ways of cultivating their farms and other occupational skills. My father mentioned this to me, and since I was anxious to improve my condition, I accepted. One of the conditions was that we should go in twos and fours. I asked my friend Flugencio to go with me but his father wouldn't allow him to go because he was attending school. So I persuaded my cousin to come along.

---

*Cordell Andersen, who served a mission to Guatemala in the 1950s, left his home in Provo, Utah, with his family in 1967 to return to Guatemala to help improve the working and living conditions of the Indians. After living among them and gaining their confidence, he began establishing classes in nutrition and sanitation, how to operate basic farm machinery, and the use of modern methods of agriculture. Daniel Choc was one of the young Indian boys who lived on Brother Andersen's 550-acre plantation and completed a six-month training course. Cordell Andersen's experiences in Guatemala are featured in "Awakening Guatemala," by Barbara Tietjen Jacobs, *Ensign*, July 1971, pp. 24-30.

With the poor roads that existed at that time,
Brother Andersen's farm was about eight hours away
from my home village. When we got there we found that
the farm was quiet, not very developed, and desolate.
My cousin became lonesome and dissatisfied, so he
returned home. Later my brother and a friend joined us,
and the work began to move forward a little faster. At
that time we didn't have anything more than a small
hand tractor, but I enjoyed learning how to operate it; I
also learned to care for chickens, pigs, and other animals.
We later acquired a real tractor, which I was taught to
operate and placed in charge of. I drove that tractor for
about a year and a half.

At the Andersen farm I also learned many things
about the gospel. When I first went there I was very
ignorant concerning the principles of the gospel of Jesus
Christ. My father, who was himself a new member, did
not know a great deal about the Church. We had held
only a few family home evenings at our house. But with
more experiences my father has learned much about the
true religion, and has been an inspiration to his family.

I have been asked what is the most important thing I
have learned since I became a member of the Church.
The thing I treasure most is that despite my not having
attended school for very long, and despite my not having
been fed and clothed properly as a young boy, and
despite my being retarded educationally, I have become
highly motivated to grow and to learn and to overcome
the obstacles of my life. Because of the Church, I have
not lost my way. I have never partaken of liquor or any
other similar things.

I feel special gratitude toward the Church for having
taught me the right way in keeping myself morally
clean. Without the Church I would never have really
learned about virtue. I don't know why, but in Indian
homes in our part of the world parents are afraid to say
anything about sexual matters. Older people do not
teach the law of chastity. The Church has taught me
clearly about chastity, about its sacredness, and about

the grievousness of perverting it in our daily lives. This is a precious blessing.

(*Postscript: On March 29, 1976, while he and a number of other fulltime Mormon missionaries were helping residents of Patzun clear away the debris from a home that had been nearly demolished in the Guatemala earthquake the previous month, Elder Daniel Choc was killed instantly by a collapsing wall. His funeral was held on March 30, 1976.*)

IV
UNTO THE ASIANS

15

TO THE KOREANS, AND ALL THE PEOPLE OF ASIA

by Elder Bruce R. McConkie

(Note: The era of change through which members of The Church of Jesus Christ of Latter-day Saints are now passing requires readjustment in attitudes and direction. As many Latter-day Saints are called upon to reach out from a Westernized church into the development of a universal kingdom of God, the peoples of Asia are of special concern. Their languages and traditions are relatively little understood in the Church at large, but with God's help members will successfully meet the challenge of bridging that cultural gap. Asians are an extraordinary people whose influence will be increasingly felt as they obtain an honorable place within the ranks of the Church. Such is the thrust of the message published here for the first time. It was originally delivered by Elder McConkie at a dinner gathering of returned Korea missionaries and their families at the Provo Utah Sharon East Stake Center on March 5, 1971. Though the audience to which it was addressed was specialized, the message is of enduring and universal importance.)

What I shall do now, if I may be guided by the Spirit, is give you some feeling of what is involved in taking the gospel of salvation to the ends of the earth,

with particular reference to Asia, and more specifically
to the great nation of Korea.

By way of comparison, let us look back to the
religious situation in the meridian of time. We are faced
with some conditions that are analogous to those that
prevailed when Jesus came and set up his church and
kingdom on this earth in the dispensation of the
meridian of time. He then had in force a particular
system so far as preaching the gospel to nations and
peoples was concerned. He had the express and pointed
requirement that the gospel was meant only for the
house of Israel, only for the literal descendants of
Abraham. He taught them, and he sent the apostles and
seventies to teach them. He laid a restriction upon them.
He did not send his missionaries to other nations of the
earth; as a matter of fact, in large measure this
requirement had been in force for generations among
the people who were the seed of Abraham and the
chosen lineage. Abraham's children made up the family
that was appointed to receive the gospel in that day and
for that time.

Then there came a day when Jesus commanded that
the gospel should go to all the world, and he erased what
had been before. He removed all restrictions of the past.
He said, in effect, "From this time, the gospel is to go to
all the world." He said it plainly and clearly and
bluntly. But his apostolic ministers had been so
completely and totally indoctrinated with the fact that
the plan of salvation was limited to a particular people
and a particular nation that they found it exceedingly
difficult to completely reverse the field and begin going
to the gentile nations and to the ends of the earth. And
so we have a New Testament account of considerable
difficulty and turmoil when Paul and Peter and others
were involved in making the transition from a day when
the gospel was limited, to the day when it went to
everyone; the transition from a church that was for a
limited group, to a world church.

Now, this change didn't occur overnight. There was
a least a quarter of a century involved, and during all

that period there were conflict, turmoil, contention, difficulty, and differences of opinion. Much of the disagreement centered around circumcision, that is, around the adoption of the total Mosaic system, circumcision being the symbol of it. Finally a world concept of the church was established.

Now we are at the beginning of an era of transition in our day that in large measure is comparable to what went on in New Testament times. In this dispensation we haven't yet taken the gospel to all the world, and yet we have revelations that require it. However, we have done the only possible thing that could have been done in this dispensation: we began the missionary work to the extent of our capacity and our ability. With a few missionaries we started out in the surrounding areas of the United States. Soon our missionaries were in Canada; then they were in England; then they spread to the nations of continental Europe; and then they went to the islands of the Pacific. And in all those places we had some impact. Yet in our revelations we are commanded to go to all nations; and so even in the early days, in an attempt to do what the Lord required, the missionaries went to India and to various nations in the nethermost parts of the Lord's vineyard. But no success, to speak of, attended any of these labors. I can remember isolated instances of conversion only. And it has gone on that way until almost the present moment in the Church.

When I was a young missionary, we boasted with some pride that there were fifteen hundred to two thousand missionaries out in the world. At the present moment [1971] we have almost 14,000 missionaries in full-time service. The Church is doubling in membership in less than a quarter of a century, and the missionary force is increasing about as rapidly as the Church membership increases. In no more than twenty years from now it will be no problem at all to have 25,000 missionaries out [this figure was reached in 1976], and forty or fifty years from now, 50,000; and seventy-five years from now, 100,000, just assuming the normal ratios of increase that are projected with the present rate of growth.

I indicate these figures to show that we are coming into a period of time when, for the first time in the history of the Church, we are beginning to get the strength to go out to the ends of the earth and fulfill in small measure now, but in large measure in due course, the requirement to take the gospel to all the people. We're making our start.

It is in our day that we're beginning in Asia, and it is in Asia where so many people are. We haven't realized this in the Church for the obvious reason that our ancestry derives from western and northern Europe. We have been a European-centered culture, as it were. And predominantly, the influence of the church has been expended in that part of the world.

I'm not intending to indicate that there will ever be a day when there will be a total swing away from the culture we have and the influence that has so far been spread. But I do want to open the door and indicate that there is going to be a major shift in emphasis as other nations come in and make their influence felt in the gospel. So, as rapidly as we have gained the power--meaning the strength, the financial means, and the personnel--the Lord has somehow had some historical events occur, events that are wholly normal, circumstances without anything seemingly miraculous being involved, that have opened up other nations to the spread of the gospel.

Asia is where the people are. The first time my wife and I went to Japan we met Brother Ted Price, who was there with the American Embassy, a faithful member of the Church. He said to me half in jest, but with a serious overtone, "When are you fellows going to quit doing missionary work with the minority groups and get over here where the people are?" The people are in Asia.

When we first went into Hong Kong, President Brent Hardy said, "Welcome to two of the four corners of the earth." He meant his mission. I said, "How many nonmembers of the Church are there in your mission?" He said, "One billion 700 million." Asia is where the people are! We have divided his mission since then--but there are still 1 billion 700 million people to whom we must preach.

We have dedicated the land of Indonesia. A little over a year ago we had twelve missionaries there. There are 131 million people in Indonesia; it is the fifth largest nation in the world.

We haven't yet come to the point where we can get to all the nations of the earth. We don't have the personnel; we don't have the strength. There aren't enough missionaries to do it. There are 840 million people who speak Mandarin, the largest number of people who speak any language in the world. We haven't done a thing yet on mainland China. But we ought to realize that the Lord meant what he said when he gave the command, speaking of the gospel that was restored through Joseph Smith, that this gospel was going to go to every nation, kindred, tongue, and people. That's literal in the full sense of the word. There is to be no nation, no kindred, no tongue, and no people who will not hear the restored gospel, as it came through Joseph Smith, and hear it before the second coming of the Son of Man.

There's a timetable, a divine timetable. We hear many sermons preached about how imminent the second coming may be—that it could be in so many years, that it will come soon because of this, that, or the other thing. I don't know when the second coming will be, but it won't be next week, and it won't be next year, and it won't be for an appreciable period of time, because it's not going to come until two things take place.

The first thing that must take place is that the restored gospel is to be preached in every nation and among every people and to those speaking every tongue. Now there is one immediate reaction to this: Can't we go on the radio and preach the gospel to Korea, or to the other nations of the earth? We certainly can, but that would have very little bearing on the real meaning of the revelation that says we must preach it to every nation, kindred, and people. The reason is the second thing that must occur before the second coming: The revelations expressly, specifically, and pointedly say that when the Lord comes the second time to usher in the millennial era, he is going to find, in every nation, kindred, and tongue, and among every people, those who are kings and queens, who will live and reign a thousand years on earth. (Revelation 5:9-10.)

That is a significant statement that puts in perspective the preaching of the gospel to the world. Yes, we can go on the radio; we can proclaim the gospel to all nations by television or other modern invention. And to the extent that we do it, so be it, it's all to the good. But that's not what is involved. What is involved is that the elders of Israel, holding the priesthood, in person have to trod the soil, eat in the homes of the people, figuratively put their arms around the honest in heart, feed them the gospel, and baptize them and confer the Holy Ghost upon them. Then these people have to progress and advance, and grow in the things of the Spirit, until they can go to the house of the Lord, until they can enter a temple of God and receive the blessings of the priesthood, out of which come the rewards of being kings and priests.

The way we become kings and priests is through the ordinances of the house of the Lord. It is through celestial marriage; it is through the guarantees of eternal life and eternal increase that are reserved for the Saints in the temples. The promise is that when the Lord comes he is going to find in every nation and kindred, among every people speaking every tongue, those who will, at that hour of his coming, have already become kings and priests. This means that they've been converted to the truth and have grown in grace and the things of the spirit to the point that they receive the same blessings in the house of the Lord that some of us have received. All this is to precede the second coming of the Son of Man.

This begins to put things in perspective, and I think we have commenced this transition period. We have commenced the quarter century of our day. There has been a transfer of the emphasis so far as the preaching of the gospel and the proclamation of the message of peace are concerned. We have commenced that period, and there are going to be some struggles and some difficulties, some prejudices and some uncertainties along the way. There are going to be members of the Church who are prejudiced against this nation or that because of the color of the people's hair, or their eyes, or their skin, or because of some social circumstance that has existed in their prior history.

The Lord's hand is in the missionary system of the Church. He works it out so that every time we have the strength to supply another 150 missionaries, we discover a place where we need another mission––and we put the additional 150 missionaries there. World events roll along with their difficulties and turmoil and war, and yet out of it all, doors are opened for the preaching of the gospel.

In Korea we had a war, and men died and their blood was shed; pride, iniquity, immorality, and all that attends war ran rampant. You might say the devil was having a field day. But the Lord hadn't turned the world over to Satan; he was still keeping control. So out of all the difficulties that occurred in Korea came the preaching of the gospel to that nation. Into the Korean conflict was woven a silver thread of grace and goodness in life. Out of the Korean war came the Church in the Korean nation. How did it come? Obviously, we had our LDS servicemen there, including many returned missionaries and active Church members. You don't have returned missionaries and Mormon elders who close their mouths. They taught the gospel to their buddies; converts were made. It was inevitable that their teachings would spill over in some measure to the native people. Thus we ended up with little groups of Korean people in the Church when the so-called peace arrived. Now there was only one thing to do, and that was to take care of the Saints. Missionaries had to go in, and the spread of the gospel began anew. Now we have 5,000 members of the Church in Korea. . . .

It is going to go like that from nation to nation and

from kingdom to kingdom. I don't have the slightest idea how we're going to get into India, or China, or some of the other nations. But it is absolutely guaranteed that we'll get there.

Just a little interesting sidelight on this. There are two Chinese languages, Mandarin and Cantonese. The people speak Mandarin in Taiwan and Nationalist China; they speak Cantonese in Hong Kong. We have a mission in Hong Kong with five thousand members, and another mission in Taiwan with five thousand members. Just by chance, we now have Saints in Hong Kong and in Taiwan whose ancestry stems from every major city on mainland China. One of these days, in the normal course of world events, something will happen to open mainland China to the gospel. And when that day comes, we will have hundreds of elders who will give anything in the world that they possess to get back to the land of their ancestors to preach the gospel and bear testimony that Joseph Smith was a prophet. The Lord opens the way and prepares these things to come to pass.

In Korea, there are 32 million people. As a matter of fact, if we had the power and the strength, we would have two missions in Korea now. [Note: A second mission was organized in 1975.] And there would be 15 or so million nonmembers in each mission. We have four missions in Japan [eight in 1978] and there are 105 million people there. When Brother Ezra Taft Benson and I were assigned to the Asian area less than three years ago, they were just organizing the fifth mission in Asia. Now we have nine. Where we had a few hundred baptisms in years gone by, we now have many thousands.

The Church is growing, and it's a very stable growth; it's a sound and good growth. Korea is the only nation on earth where we baptize more men than we baptize women, and that has a lot of good, wholesome aspects to it. We're getting a very high type of people everywhere in Asia. It would be interesting to know how it came about that the blood of Israel became scattered into the Asian parts of the earth. We can really only speculate about this. It is my judgment that we'll never really know how this came about until the day we begin to receive revelation on it. This may well mean that it won't be until the millennial era arrives; but the means by which it was brought to pass is not nearly as important as the fact that it exists.

Those people who have been given patriarchal blessings from Korea and elsewhere have been told by the spirit of inspiration that they are of the house of Israel. There isn't any question at all about that. This means that in their veins flows the same blood that flows in our veins. It's not just the single fact that God has made of one blood all the nations of men, that they should dwell on all the face of the earth. It is the fact that the house of Israel, the choicest and most select and favored blood of the earth, has been spread everywhere. And we're getting that blood into the Church in Korea and in Asia, and I'm sure we'll find it in all the untouched nations of the earth as rapidly as we get into them.

Last year there were six Korean couples who were able to go through the temple and receive their blessings; another seven couples are scheduled to go this year. That's a small beginning. That's the beginning of doing things that will make kings and priests in the Korean nation to prepare a people there for the second coming of the Son of Man. What we do in the spread of the gospel to that nation will have eternal overtones. It won't be something that is limited to the brief span of mortality. It is going to affect people for all eternity.

In order to completely and totally fulfill the revelation that people are entitled to have the gospel taught to them in their own tongue and in their own language, the eventual destiny is to have the native people do the missionary work. This means Koreans teaching Koreans. We can't do it until they become strong enough, and they can't become strong enough without our help. Interestingly, in this respect, in the Japan Central Mission 41 of the 165 missionaries who are now serving are native Japanese. One missionary in four of those on missions there is a native person. Nearly every one is a convert to the Church. Someday there are going to be hundreds and hundreds of native Koreans, in their own tongue and in their own language, teaching their own kindred and gaining the experience that will qualify them for positions of leadership in stakes of Zion that will be organized.

There can't be any question at all but what there will be stakes in Korea. We just created our first stake in Asia; it was organized in Tokyo—four thousand members in six wards—and the day it was organized, every stake and ward officer had been to the temple and had had his own endowments. Every one of them was a full tithepayer. This is more than you can say for some stakes that are in the shadows of the temples, as it were.* As in Japan, so in Korea. There will be stakes of Zion. Someday there will be a stake in Seoul and one in Pusan, and who knows where else.

Now I don't know whether there will be a temple in Korea, but I can say this: it wouldn't surprise me in the slightest to see, in the lives of us here, the establishment of a temple there. The gospel can explode and expand and spread that rapidly. And I do know this in principle: that whenever there is a large enough congregation of Saints to justify these things, somehow the Lord opens a way and inspires the brethren, and the eventuality comes to pass. Someday, assuming the growth that there ought to be, we'll need to have facilities so the people can get their own endowments and be sealed for eternity.

Those of you here who are the parents of missionaries in Korea should, in my judgment, take pride in the field of service where your sons are. They are laying a foundation for a great work, and they are working with a choice and favored people. Brother Palmer wrote on his program here tonight three distinguishing characteristics of Koreans. As I read these distinguishing characteristics,

---

*As of September 1, 1978, there were seven stakes in Japan.

I thought to myself, these ought to be the three distinguishing characteristics of Latter-day Saints everywhere: (1) hospitality, (2) family-centeredness and a great love for children, and (3) love for learning and education.

Koreans have a different background than we have, of course, which is of no moment to the Lord. We have a different social and cultural background than the Jews have or than Abraham or Moses had. And who knows what cultural background and educational circumstances prevailed before the flood, in those families of nations that had the gospel. The cultural background that we've had is of no moment. What counts is whether we receive the gospel of Jesus Christ and live its laws. We're not trying to change the cultural background for anyone. I think what President George Albert Smith used to say, in principle, is an ideal guide for us. In talking of missionary work, he used to say, "Keep every good thing that you have, and then let us add the further light and knowledge that has come to us by revelation."

Our customs are good for us and we have been trained in them. It is no different to have different social customs than it is to have different languages. You speak the language you inherit. And the Lord knows all languages. As far as he is concerned, it is just as good to speak Mandarin as it is to speak English. On this basis, we are only trying to take truth to people throughout the world, truth in addition to what they have. Certainly, there are false things among every nation and in every culture. And what is false, we want to reject; and good and proper thinking people among them want to reject it also. But whatever is appropriate and good we want to preserve. It ought to be one of the aims of the Korean people to preserve their culture, to keep their own dances and their own dress and their own mores and ways of life alive, as long as they are not inharmonious with gospel principles. This is what the Church is saying to the Koreans and to all the people of Asia today.

May the Lord bless us one and all as we seek to serve him and carry forward his holy purposes in the nations of the earth, and especially among his other children in Asia. Let us labor to find the lost sheep of Israel who are among them. In helping to build up the kingdom in that part of the earth, we shall bless ourselves and all those whose lives we touch. The Lord has already blessed and prospered those who have been chosen to labor in this special part of his vineyard, and he will continue to do so in a marvelous and abundant manner. The work in which we are engaged is true and it will triumph. God's work does not fail. Such is my testimony, in the name of Jesus Christ. Amen.

16
THE CHURCH
IN SOUTHEAST ASIA

In 1920, Asia's one billion people were fifty-five percent of the earth's total population of 1.9 billion. Half a century later, in 1970, Asia's 2.1 billion were fifty-seven percent of the earth's total population of 3.6 billion. The Asian population in 1970 was larger than the total population of the earth in 1920.

The most obvious problem facing the Church in Asia is how to reach all these people. Yet, it is not simply a problem of arithmetic; rather it is one of becoming prepared to face new complexities of language, culture, and race. The challenge is perhaps best illustrated in Southeast Asia, where the Church has only recently organized independent missions in Thailand, Indonesia, and the Philippine Islands, and in widely separated proselyting "stations" known collectively as the Singapore Mission.

The map of Southeast Asia appears to have been drawn by Procrustes, that mythical Greek who was noted for his arbitrary and ruthless disregard of individual differences and special circumstances. National boundaries, which to a certain degree are the remains of

former foreign invasion, are superimposed in apparent
disregard for native geographic, ethnic, and cultural patterns. For Southeast Asia is not a unity. It comprises a
dazzling variety of peoples, nationalities, beliefs, values,
and religious forms and of social, economic, and political
patterns.

Southeast Asia has been influenced for millennia by
the great cultures of the Han Chinese from the north
and the Hindus of India on the west. Buddhism, Hinduism, the faith of Islam, and the ethics of Confucius are
all ancient additions. The cultures and economics of the
native peoples changed with the migrations, the expan-
sions and contractions, and the increases and declines of
the successive intruders.

Centuries of colonial and imperial control brought
further diversity and changes to what was already there.
Spain and Portugal established enduring regimes in
certain areas. The Philippines, initially a Spanish area
ruled through viceroys in the Americas, eventually became a colony of the United States. Indonesia was ruled
by the Netherlands; Indochina (Cambodia, Laos, and
Vietnam) by the French; Malaya and some island areas
by the British. Thailand has remained politically independent. Some Japanese have moved southward in
ancient and colonial times, but the rule of Imperial
Japan reached Southeast Asia only briefly during World
War II.

Ethnic migration during the twentieth century in
Southeast Asia has been extensive, particularly in the
Philippines, where Mormonism has met with almost
dramatic success in numbers of convert baptisms since
missionary work began in the early 1960s. In Malaysia,
where organized proselyting has not yet begun, rapid
change has also characterized the demography of the
principal regions of Malaya, Sabah, and Sarawak. The
present ethnic composition of the nation and its urban
and rural distribution result from a long history of heavy
immigration and from important ethnic differences in
birth and death patterns. In 1970 Malaysia was still very
much a rural nation. In more highly urbanized West

Malaysia, less than a third of the population lived in towns of 10,000 or more persons. In East Malaysia, less than a sixth lived in towns. In the nation as a whole, only eight towns had more than 75,000 people. While the largest towns were growing more quickly than the rural areas, recent urban growth rates do not indicate massive rural-to-urban migration.

Indonesia, the most populous country in Southeast Asia, had a reported 1971 population exceeding 119 million. The true population was perhaps greater by six or seven million. According to U.S. Bureau of Census estimates, the crude birth rate stood at 44 and the death rate at 19 per 1,000 in 1970. The death rate, high by Asian standards, reflects the per capita declines in food production and the reemergence of malaria, smallpox, tuberculosis, and plague during the 1970s as well as the prevalence of cholera and the deterioration of public health services. Yet Indonesia, where Mormon missionary work has met with promising results in its initial phases, is only one example of the tremendous economic and health care needs of the people in Southeast Asia. If the needs of people in neighboring India, Bangladesh, and Pakistan are taken into consideration, these problems are magnified manyfold.

The labors and sufferings of Latter-day Saint missionaries in India, Siam (Thailand), Burma, and adjacent areas and islands of South and Southeast Asia during the mid-nineteenth century are rather well marked in the annals of Church history and in a number of other studies. But these were largely short-lived individual exercises in bearing witness and affirming commitments to the restored gospel, not organized programs directed toward the development of a church that would be responsive to the needs and conditions of the local people. It wasn't until well after the end of World War II that the Church was in a position to begin doing that.

Soren F. Cox, a professor of English and linguistics at Brigham Young University, lived with his family in Singapore during 1970-72 while he administered a program of teaching English as a second language at Nanyang

University. In the following pages, he provides interesting and stimulating insights into what may lie ahead. His experience among the peoples of Southeast Asia has opened new horizons and given focus to new issues that call for the attention of the Church. In his work in Singapore, Professor Cox discovered that even English is not the same in Southeast Asia, where idiosyncracies abound. Here are his views, based upon oral interviews first recorded in the early summer of 1975, as he prepared to leave to preside over the Singapore Mission; he reviewed them again after his release in 1978.

17

ONE BANQUET, MANY FOODS
by Soren F. Cox

The Singapore Tourist Promotion Board calls Singapore "Instant Asia." About 75 percent of the people in Singapore are Chinese, with their several languages and a variety of religious groups, including Buddhists, and Confucian ancestor worshippers; however, many young Singaporeans call themselves "free thinkers." About 15 percent of the people are Malay. The Malay people are primarily Muslim (Islamis) in religion and their language is closely related to Indonesian. Nearly 8 percent of the people are Indian, mostly South Indian, with a few Sikhs and Punjabis. These Indians are primarily Hindu in religion, and south Indian in culture and language.

Singapore is a country with many languages and many cultures represented; in it are represented the peoples who reside in the various countries that are in the Singapore Mission. The mission was formed in October/November 1969; within a few months the two branches of the church in Singapore numbered about 350 members. By 1975 there were almost 500 members, about two-thirds of whom were Chinese and Indian;

one-third were Americans, Australians, and New
Zealanders who were in Singapore for business, military,
and other purposes.

Singapore, the headquarters of the mission, is both a
country and a city. The president of the Singapore
Mission works with the members in Brunei; Malaysia,
which includes the Malaysian Peninsula south of
Thailand and two states, Sarawak and Sabah, on North
Borneo; Sri Lanka, formerly known as Ceylon; and the
subcontinent of India. This constitutes an enormous
geographical area with a population of more than
650,000,000 people.

The area is an interesting challenge to the Church
because not only is it considered to be a developing part
of the world, belonging to the so-called third world, but
all of these countries also have a background of
colonialism. That is, all of them were previously ruled by
the British. This background has created some
conditions that are favorable to the Church's work, but
it produces others that are not. One of the favorable
conditions is that English is widely used as a second
language. Therefore, it is possible to go into most of
these countries and use English in the major cities and
even to some extent in the countryside.

A disadvantage is that all of the countries are fairly
new nations. In terms of gaining its independence from
colonial rule, the oldest is the Republic of India, which
was founded in 1948. The newest country is Singapore,
which achieved its separate independence as a nation in
1965. Brunei still retains ties with England, with the
British providing the defense and conducting the
international affairs for this small country.

Another problem for Mormon missionary work is
that these countries also have backgrounds of internal
religious, political, and cultural conflicts. The
particularly sensitive problem of the impact and role of
Western culture is perhaps accentuated more in
Singapore than in the other countries. In that small
country of 2.5 million people, mostly Chinese, the prime
minister visited Nanyang University (a Chinese

university) and told the students that they must learn English; they must become bilingual to compete for the best jobs in Singapore. Fearing the effects of such an emphasis on English, many in his audience might resist his pressure. However, this is the reasoning of the government: English is the language of technology, of business, and of tourism, all of which are important in the economy of Singapore. Therefore, the prime minister said, in effect, "If, as a very small nation, we are to continue our existence and maintain our freedom politically and economically, our citizens must know English." However, many of the people fear that students who learn English will also adopt the more negative aspects of Western customs and culture.

Until 1975, the students at Nanyang University were studying in the Chinese language, while some of their brothers and sisters and friends at Singapore University were studying in English. Frequently the students at Nanyang talked about the differences between them and their colleagues at Singapore University, noting that those attending Nanyang were retaining the Chinese culture, the traditions of their parents, while those studying at Singapore University "do not respect their parents as they should. They are not as moral as we are. They do not work as hard as we do. They do not dress in the traditional patterns."

The men at Nanyang University dress neatly in shirts and trousers, and the women wear dresses––no slacks or pantsuits. Men and women walk on opposite sides of the street; they sit on opposite sides of the classrooms; they study long hours and rely a great deal on memorization in learning subjects. On the other hand, many of their compatriots at Singapore University date as in Western cultures, and wear the clothing and the long-hair styles typical of Western college students. The traditionalists see in the behavior of the students at Singapore University an abandoning of traditional cultures and a decaying in morality.

The problem of keeping Chinese culture while learning English as a means of access to economic prosperity has been a source of tension for the students as well as a problem for the government. That the government has tried to walk a very tight line is illustrated by the experience of an acquaintance of mine. He was the editor of a Chinese newspaper in Singapore. Because he too vigorously defended the Chinese way and the Chinese language (and was too favorable to Communist China), he was arrested by the police and taken to prison. Singapore still has a law on the books that goes back to the Communist troubles of the fifties and early sixties, which says a man can be put in prison if he excites community strife between the races or the religions.

Another significant challenge facing the Church is the fact that many people in Asia view The Church of Jesus Christ of Latter-day Saints as a Western church. In some ways this view contributes to the reluctance some countries express to allowing the Mormon missionaries—or any foreign Christian missionaries—to proselyte within their boundaries. In India, at the time of the discussion of the constitution in 1948 (actually, discussion of the matter goes back to the nineteenth century), the question arose, "Should proselyting be allowed?" The Hindu religion, of course, does not believe in proselyting. Gandhi said he did not believe in conversion. And Hinduism is an inclusive religion that is a combination of several different forms of belief, so many Hindus look with a jaundiced eye at the practice of proselyting. Nevertheless, the constitution does stipulate that proselyting is legal; however, the law does not allow foreign missionaries to exceed a quota that was established at the time of independence. In 1948, at the time the Indian constitution was adopted, there were no Mormon missionaries in India; therefore, the Church does not have missionaries in that country.

Another kind of difficulty that we are not fully accustomed to thinking of in the Western world is created by attitudes toward language. The Singapore Mission is a polyglot, or multilingual, mission. In India alone there are fourteen official languages. Among those languages are some that belong to the same language family as English (the Indo-European family), but there are also the Dravidian languages of southern India, which belong to an entirely different group. Church materials have not been printed or translated in any of the languages that are used in India nor in many of the languages used throughout the Singapore mission.

Language differences have been a highly charged political issue throughout Southeast Asia. In all the countries in the area, English—though it was hated as the language of the colonial master—is widely used. The somewhat paradoxical attitude that frequently exists toward the use of English is manifest in the statement made by an official of the Malaysian Ministry of Education at a conference on English as a second language, held in Kuala Lumpur, the capital of Malaysia. He said, "We want to learn English, but we don't want to learn English." And this is the real problem—simultaneous attraction-repulsion. Many Asians feel the need to learn English because it is the commercial, technological, and, in some ways, cultural window to much of the world. But they also want to promote their local language because it gives them national pride and an identification with their culture, with their own native land. Malaysia has resolved the issue by passing a law decreeing that by 1983 all public-supported teaching in Malaysia from kindergarten through university must be in Malay. A number of teachers do not know Malay; many Indian teachers speak the Tamil language and English, and many Chinese speak Chinese and/or English. By 1983 all of these teachers have to learn Malay.

India is a more complex example of linguistic problems. Though there are fourteen official languages that can be the language of government and education in the different states, English has been the common language used for communication among educated people throughout India. Shortly after independence the government decreed that Hindi would be the official language of India. This led to bloody rioting in southern

India. The Tamil-speaking Indians resisted fiercely; they were much more willing to learn English than they were Hindi, because the Hindi speakers had been their enemies for many centuries. Even today, language differences are highly emotional problems in India.

Language has been a volatile issue in Malaysia, Singapore, Sri Lanka, and India. It has been used by political parties as a vehicle for gaining power. If we Latter-day Saints begin teaching the gospel in the regional languages of some of these countries, what are the implications in terms of our relationship with the federal government, which has decreed a certain language shall be the national tongue? Language policies are very important; we must exercise great care as we begin work in the different countries where language is a controversial issue.

Another difficult issue we face in South and Southeast Asia relates to the religions of the various countries. In Malaysia and Pakistan, and in some parts of India, there are large numbers of Muslims. In Singapore and Malaysia there are laws that make it illegal to proselyte Muslims. Restrictions of various kinds exist in other countries. The majority of the 600,000,000 people in India are Hindu. In Nepal, which is also predominantly Hindu, not only is it forbidden to proselyte, but it is also illegal to change religion.

One of the problems that arises as a result of these religious differences is that as people from these countries join the Church, we need to ask what they must leave behind in terms of the previous cultures and traditions and what they can bring with them into the Church from their previous cultures and traditions.

Perhaps an experience in Singapore will illustrate the kinds of cultural-religious problems we face. A young Indian convert became very active in missionary work, and in two years she introduced about twenty people to the Church. She converted her boyfriend, a Hindu, to the Church. They wanted to have a church wedding, but the father of the young man was so upset that the son had become a Christian that he said, "All right, you

can defy me and marry a Christian, but if you do not
marry in the Hindu temple, I'll not arrange marriages
for any of your sisters." In a culture where marriages are
arranged by the father, this was a serious threat to the
welfare of the poor unmarried daughters in the family.
Therefore, the young LDS couple, both converts to the
Church, were forced to go to the Hindu temple to be
married in accordance with a very elaborate Hindu
ceremony.

Another young Indian convert in Singapore, whose
father was a Hindu, faced the problem of having her
father arrange a marriage for her with a man who was
almost twenty years older than she. She did not want to
marry the man. She finally agreed to discuss her feelings
with her father. (This, of course, isn't something that a
girl would normally do, but her father was an
intelligent, educated man.) To her surprise, he agreed to
call the marriage off. However, within three weeks he
had arranged for her to marry a young Tamil teacher in
Singapore. This arrangement was acceptable to her. The
young woman did not see her husband until the day of
the wedding, a typical practice in that culture. Is this an
acceptable practice for these people as they come into
the Church? Is it acceptable for them to continue the
practice of arranged marriages and having a dowry paid
by the father of the bride to the father of the groom?
What is mandated by the gospel and what is simply
Western culture?

Another problem in southern India is related to
music. There are four little groups of the Church in and
near the city of Coimbatore. In three of the groups are
people who do not use the organ and the piano as
traditional musical instruments. They are accustomed to
a different kind of musical notation and use different
kinds of instruments. As these people come into the
Church, do we require them to obtain organs and pianos
as their musical instruments? Do we insist that they
adopt worship songs with a new system of musical
notation and that they learn the hymns with organ and
piano accompaniment, or is it possible to translate the

message of the hymn into another kind of music? They
customarily use reed instruments, a large number of
string instruments, and, of course, percussion
instruments. So what do they do about music when they
come into the Church?

For the Church, the problem is, what is basic in the
gospel that they must accept and what is really just
Western culture, United States culture, or even Utah
culture? What must we ask them to accept and what are
they free to reject?

The problem manifests itself in many ways. Some
time ago some Americans were serving as dance directors
in the branches in Singapore. For an activity night they
organized a square dance. The young people had a lot of
fun and it would be appropriate to say, "Here are
typical dances of people who live in American West,
interesting to learn but culturally different." But often
that is not the assumption conveyed to new converts in
Asia. Rather, we seem to imply that "square dances are
what Mutual is all about." We must be more sensitive to
the cultures of the local people.

In terms of effective communication, one of our
challenges is to see that the language of the Church
manuals and other instructional materials is carefully
scrutinized not only for the obvious culture cues, but
also for the more subtle ones. For example, one manual
that we received in Singapore mentioned "dime." Well,
"dime" doesn't happen to be a part of Singaporean
coinage, and it posed a problem. And sometimes certain
assumptions are made that everyone dates the way
young people do in the United States. When such
assumptions are made, teachers in Asia have problems
handling the lessons.

Another consideration is that even when the Saints
in some countries have learned English, they use a brand
of English peculiar to their area. For example, in the
Philippines, is there such a thing as standard Filipino
English, which is different from British English or from
American English? In other words, educated Filipino
English may have certain patterns that deviate from the

patterns of American and British English.

This is true in Singapore as well. There are also many different varieties of Indian English. The Indian English in southern India, where the native language is Tamil, has certain characteristics that differ from the English spoken in northern India, where the speakers have a different language background. We Latter-day Saints must adjust to the fact that English is not the same around the world, that there are differences between British English, American English, Filipino English, Singaporean English, and different types of Indian English. This poses serious problems for manual writers, even for those who write the manuals in English for English-speaking members.

The Church has a bright future in South and Southeast Asia. In Singapore and Malaysia, we haven't yet attracted many older people to the Church, but we have converted a number of younger people. In that part of the world the older traditions are being shaken by confrontation with Western technology. They are being modified or abandoned, which creates a vacuum. Many young people don't want to adopt Western traditions, but they have abandoned some of the traditions of their fathers. For many of these young people the gospel offers a solid ground on which they can establish a life that is meaningful and moral, but not the permissive society so often identified with British and American cultures.

In Singapore we have two strong English-speaking branches and a good deal of able local leadership. We are now allowed to have only one foreign missionary—that is all that the government will allow. Strong corps of local missionaries must be built up. In Malaysia there is one Church group in Kuala Lumpur, composed primarily of Malaysian Chinese and a few American families.

In India, the Church is incorporated and recognized, but because of legal proscriptions, we are not allowed to send in foreign missionaries. There are four small groups of some 180 native members in southern India, near Coimbatore. Three of the groups consist of farm workers

and laborers, mostly illiterate. The members in
Coimbatore are literate; most of them speak some
English, but their first language is Tamil. These groups
are supervised by Paul Thirurthuvidoss, an elder in the
Melchizedek Priesthood. In New Delhi we have a small
group composed of a few Indian families and a few
American families. There are also American families
scattered in Madras and other places. The total
membership in India is about 250.

Experience in Asia emphasizes the great challenge of
achieving racial harmony within the Church. The
problem and the prospects can be illustrated by a Junior
Sunday School class in Singapore. The class consists of a
Chinese-Indian girl, Americans, Singaporeans, New
Zealanders, Australians, and Chinese--children with all
shades of skin from very light to dark, and many
different facial structures and other differences in
appearance. This group illustrates the diversity that will
be the linguistic, cultural, and racial makeup of the
Church in coming years. In Singapore these highly
diversified groups are associating together in friendship
and love--the kind of development that must come to
the Church as we reach out to all peoples and bring
them into one gospel and one church.

We are seeking to make all people alike in the sense
that they come to worship one God and to love one
another. We hold firmly to the doctrine of one faith and
one baptism, but in terms of clothing and food, we must
accept diversity. We must accept Chinese food, Malay
food, Indian food, and, of course, American and English
food. In Singapore the fare laid before us is diverse,
tempting, and tantalizing. We all come together for one
banquet, but we all bring those diverse elements of our
own culture. Our colors are different, our languages are
different, and our dress is different, but we are united in
worshipping one God and in fellowshipping together.
Indeed, the Church prepares one banquet with many
foods.

18

A JAPANESE SEARCH FOR IDENTITY

Since Brigham Young's days, Utah-centered Mormons have tried to understand the Japanese. But the barriers in the past were too great. Japan was far removed geographically from the Utah Zion, and the religion of its people was even farther removed ideologically from the tradition through which the western Saints had come. The Japanese were a pagan people, alien in religion as they were in race in the view of the Utah Mormons.

The end of World War II marked the beginning of a new era of phenomenal growth for the Church in Japan. For the Church at large, the Japanese represented a new kind of convert. For the Japanese, joining the Church of Jesus Christ posed such extraordinary new dilemmas concerning themselves and their newly discovered faith as these: What happens to a Japanese who joins the Church? What happens to his perceptions (a) of himself and his ethnicity and culture, (b) of other Japanese, (c) of Americans, and (d) of the world at large? Are questions of identity magnified or resolved by joining the Church? What do the life experiences of Japanese converts reveal concerning Japanese character and ways of thought that might in time influence or enhance the Church, or that might help clarify the relationship of the restored gospel to Japanese traditional culture?

These are fundamental questions with which the Masao Watabe family of Japan, along with many other Japanese, have been faced since joining the Church in recent years. Masao was the first of his family to become a baptized Latter-day Saint. His concerns were those of a traditional, patriotically loyal citizen of the Japanese Empire during the war years whose primary concern after joining the Church was how to retain a continuity with the past that would be compatible with the principles of his newly discovered Christian faith. His zealous excitement with the doctrines and history of Mormonism is offset by a compelling desire to make it relevant to his ethnicity as a Japanese. The dilemma is how to depart from the past without breaking from it; how to move forward into a new world of ideas and experiences without repudiating his own ancestral heritage. Finding himself mentally alienated but emotionally tied to his own past, he is fervently determined to become a new creature in Christ, but to do so as a self-respecting Japanese.

His story is suffused with another dominating theme: man in nature. Masao Watabe's intimacy with nature is impressive and very Japanese. To him, nature evokes a deep sense of spirituality: in waterfalls, lakes, and streams; white clouds and blue skies, shadows and sunshine, sunrise and sunset; plant and animal life. At the baptism of a son in Sendai, he recalls, "Clean water was flowing alongside a mountain which was covered with green trees, grass and some wild flowers. Birds were singing and seemed to be praising Masakazu's eternal birth. Everything was so beautiful that we imagined we were at the Susquehanna River when John the Baptist appeared to Joseph Smith and Oliver Cowdery." When he visited Nauvoo, Illinois, he recalls, "as my blood was sucked by a swarm of mosquitoes, I remembered how the Lord shed his blood on the cross." In Arizona, "the beautiful saguaro cactus flowers disappeared and instead we saw white birch trees; they seemed like virgins wearing white robes standing on the hills to welcome us."

In Masao there is what might appear to many Westerners a surprisingly emotional and spiritual approach to life, what the philosopher Hajime Nakamura calls "the irrationalistic tendencies of the Japanese" to lay emphasis upon the intuitive, fluid, incipient character of events; a fondness for simple symbolic expressions; a tendency to neglect logical, objective rules; and a way of thinking in which a human event "is not a purely personal event but an event having some value and emotional significance to the broader spheres of human relations." (*Ways of Thinking of Eastern People: India-China-Tibet-Japan* [Honolulu: East-West Press Center, 1964], p. 414.)

In all this Masao Watabe typifies traditional Japanese ways of thought that in modern times have rapidly given way to more rational and pragmatic concerns. Indeed, in aesthetic sensitivity he may seem old-fashioned.

Another striking feature in his life—one that seems to be characteristic of Japanese Latter-day Saints generally—is the capacity for total commitment. Although some of his views might make younger Japanese feel uneasy, believing that he is not representative of their new generation, Masao Watabe typifies a demonstrated Japanese capacity for thorough commitment to a cause. His total submission to the will of the Lord and his singlemindedness in standing up for the Church, in defending its principles, and in sacrificing for the accomplishment of its goals are traits of Japanese character that have found widespread expression in a variety of ways.

In Masao Watabe two world views converge. One of the most fascinating threads in his life's story is the manifestation of ways in which this has been realized. Having joined the Church, he was introduced to new frames of reference. Within the Church, and among some other Western people outside the Church, God, his revelation in Christ, and the goodness that comes from obeying their commandments are the "concept clearing-centers" through which practically all else in language, visual symbols, and modes of culture must pass and be evaluated. The absolute is outside nature and is universal. In traditional Japan, however, the dominating theme is acceptance of the physical world itself as absolute because of a disposition to lay greater emphasis upon intuitive concrete events rather than upon universals. By joining the Church, Brother Watabe represents a new intermingling of aesthetics and ethics. Nature is still a synonym of beauty and fundamental in his life; but in the restored gospel, the beautiful is also true and good, and this good leads one's mind to God and his goodness (that is, salvation) to man.

Masao Watabe's commitment to God now transcends all other considerations; and in joining the Church, his Japanese identity is not threatened because the cares of this world are of only incidental interest. Yet, paradoxically, such resolution seemed easier for Masao than for his children. Masao was born and reared outside the Church. His children were practically born and reared within it. As young members living in Japan under Japanese conditions they could not avoid feelings of ambivalence toward the American influences of the Church, and this sensitivity was later sharpened and at last resolved through direct encounter with American culture in the United States.

Growing up in the Church in Japan, the Watabe children faced decisions about friends, education, nationality, and marriage, that their father himself had never faced. For them, their religious faith created a special complex of new variables in their lives that critically influenced both their self-image and their view of Japan and the world. Thus, as a child Masakazu was embarrassed in trying to explain to his playmates his associations with Americans in Sendai; as a teenager he was puzzled by a new awareness that a Mormon Japanese is different from all other Japanese. And, as a houseboy for American missionaries living on the premises of the

Yokohama Branch, he was jolted by a new understanding of the power of the gospel in his life—that, much like an extraordinary prism, it can reflect and improve upon traditional patterns of thought.

Masakazu has also been perplexed by the concept of a "chosen people," and he wrestles with questions of exactly how the Japanese fit in with the overall design of God. His decision to attend Brigham Young University added new fire to the problem. At the BYU, for the first time in his life, he belonged to an ethnic minority, while the Church itself was the majority. After considerable searching, Masakazu has discovered that his identity as a Mormon outdistances all other conceptions of himself.

As a Hawaiian *sansei* (third-generation Japanese-American), Faith Okawa Watabe has a view of the world that is different from that of a Japanese born in Japan. Her husband, Masahisa, began his search for identity in Japan, in a home where Japanese language and customs were followed. Faith's view of herself, of Japan, and of the world is as an American Mormon of Japanese descent.

Adney Y. Komatsu, the first Latter-day Saint of Japanese ancestry to become a General Authority and the first Mormon *nisei* (second-generation Japanese-American) ever assigned to serve as a mission president in Japan, has suggested that self-identity can be a very real problem for Japanese-Americans who return to the land of their ancestors. During the initial years of his own first assignment in Tokyo, he recalls that though he looked native and tried hard to appear native, his foreign accent and mannerisms rather readily exposed his foreignness.

For *nisei* Americans, identity within American society has also been difficult and often complicated at times by prejudices. During World War II they were forced to live in sequestered compounds because their loyalty and patriotism were held in question. This was an agonizing experience for all Japanese, but especially for the young American *nisei,* who felt a strong loyalty and commitment to the United States.

Faith's story is one of the power of the restored gospel in helping her sort out what in her environment must be rejected and what must be accepted in order for her to lead a successful, happy life. It is a beautiful account of ambition and upward mobility among a Hawaiian Japanese family as it fully embraces the Church. Here are signs not only of cultural differences between Japanese Hawaiians and other Americans of Hawaii, but also of differences between *nisei* and *sansei* members in Hawaii and the mainland United States and Japanese members in Hawaii. Faith's story is primarily an affirmation of pride in her identity as a Japanese-American Latter-day Saint and the binding power of the gospel in her life. Through it she has discovered a fundamental capacity to "love all kinds of Japanese, and other people too."

Here, then, are the stories of three Latter-day Saints, all descended from Japanese heritage and traditions, and each representing very different and diverse problems and mores. Each of these Saints—Masao Watabe, Masakazu Watabe, and Faith Watabe—has had to come to a personal realization of the overriding influence of the gospel, which transcends all other considerations of culture, heritage, race, and background and binds each of them into the eternal family of God.

19
MASAO WATABE'S STORY

I was born on June 6, 1914, at Keikanzan, a small
town in South Manchuria, China, but I am a Japanese.
My father participated in the Japanese-Russian War
during 1904 and 1905. After the war he had returned to
his native land, Fukushima Prefecture, in the northern
part of the Japanese island of Honshu. However, his
ancestors were farmers and it was a tradition that the
first son inherit most of the family property and land
after his father's death. Since my father was the third
son, he couldn't expect to receive an inheritance, so he
decided to emigrate to a new place of opportunity, the
United States. But since he did not have sufficient funds
he went instead to Manchuria, where he was employed
by the South Manchurian Railroad Company.

After a few years a marriage was arranged, and my
mother came from his native land to be married to him.
They reared twelve children, three daughters and nine
sons, the same number as father Jacob in the Old
Testament. Truly we were a big family, and since I was
the second son, I always had to take care of my younger
brothers and sisters. I made good grades in school and

planned to go to the university after graduation from high school, but my father asked me to work and help him educate my younger brothers. So I was employed by the Manchurian Central Bank in 1932.

While I was working in the bank, I sent part of my salary each month to my younger brother for his school costs; but after six months he died, and my father permitted me to save money for my own further education.

After I had saved part of my salary for about one more year I enrolled in the Institute of the Japan-Russia Association, intending to study Russian. I had mastered the Chinese language and wanted to learn one more foreign language. Also, at that time I loved to read the works of Tolstoy, the great Russian Christian. I greatly desired to read his books in his native language. Much later, after I became a Mormon, I was surprised to learn that Tolstoy is reported to have once prophesied that the time would come when the Mormon Church would grow throughout the world, since he believed our church is the same as the primitive church, and he was excommunicated from the Orthodox Church in his old age because he insisted that the primitive church was the only true church.

In college, I stayed with a Russian family in Harbin, Manchuria, and they used to take me to their Orthodox church, but I wasn't converted to Christianity since I had been a faithful member of one of the Shinto sects and was still a typical Japanese.

After I graduated from college in 1938, I was chosen by the Japanese Foreign Office to study abroad and was dispatched to Peking to study Chinese for three years. Before leaving I was married to the younger sister of my late classmate whom I had converted into my sect of Shintoism.

After the Manchurian incident occurred in 1931, the Japanese army occupied all of Manchuria and a new Manchurian government was established with the help of the Japanese army. After the Sino-Japanese war of 1937, the Japanese army occupied North China and began to occupy the entire east coast from north to south.

At this time Japanese nationalism was very strong and the ideological slogan was "Hakko-Ichiu-no-Seishin," which means "eight corners under one roof" or to have "the whole world in one home." And as I was a nationalist or patriotic Japanese while studying in Peking, I tried to foster this ideology among the Chinese students. We organized a Japan-China Students Association and met together to study and discuss Japanese ideas, and sometimes we played together, but we never really understood each other since we Japanese students were such strong nationalists.

After three years' study of Chinese in Peking I became a Chinese interpreter and worked at the Peking Japanese Embassy for about half a year. Then I was called to Tokyo to work at the Foreign Office of the Japanese Government.

On December 8 that year, the second World War broke out. We were told the United States had attacked us first. All the Japanese, including myself, were very angry at the Americans, thinking they were the aggressors. In 1943 I was drafted, but after I had served just one year as an officer candidate, Japan surrendered and the war was ended. Since I had been such a dedicated nationalist I was very discouraged at that time, and lost all confidence and hope, and felt no desire to live on. Many of my comrades and former classmates had been killed on the battlefield. I felt isolated and lonely, and wandered in darkness for several years.

In October 1945, I was transferred to the Sendai Liaison Office from the Tokyo Foreign Office, and early in 1947, while I was working there, I was asked to teach Chinese in the Tohoku (Northern Honshu) Foreign Language Night School. I worked three nights a week as a Chinese teacher at this school. At the school a Catholic father was teaching English, and while we waited in the teachers' room for our lesson time we talked and became acquainted.

When I talked with him, especially about the religion of Jesus Christ, I felt good in my heart, and I asked many questions concerning Christianity. As I listened to his answers my heart, which had been struggling in the darkness, gradually became enlightened, and it seemed to me the Lord's voice began to whisper into it. Sometimes the priest took me to his home and his church, and I enjoyed staying with him. One day he took me to a hill in the suburbs of Sendai and said, "We will build a boy's town here on this hill. Will you come to work for us?" He added, "We will build a big building and receive orphans."

Then I asked, "How many orphans will you take in?"

He answered, "Perhaps nine. It makes no difference how many orphans we take in; the important thing is that we can carry out Catholic worship services in this building."

I was discouraged hearing this answer, since it seemed to me they were interested only in their own worship and didn't care much about the welfare and happiness of the children.

After the priest was transferred to Germany I quit going to the Catholic Church. During the summer vacation the school at which I was teaching opened a Bible class and an American G.I. named Preston came from the army camp to teach. I attended and was very much impressed by his noble character and powerful preaching. But after only one month this class was closed and he didn't come anymore. Then I heard that at one of the mission schools, Tohoku Gakuin University, there was a Bible class every Sunday morning. I went to this university and found a wonderful Bible class, which I attended continuously for almost a year. The teacher was a Methodist minister's wife, and she used to take me to her church after her class.

Soon I began to attend the Methodist Church. A Free Methodist lady missionary visited my home and began a Bible class there, and some friends and neighbors gathered to hear her teach.

The minister and his wife advised me to be baptized into their church, and I was thinking seriously about converting, but as I studied more about their faith I had too many unanswered questions. I asked them about the Virgin Mary and miracles that the Lord had performed. They just said, "It's up to you." I was discouraged to learn they had no confidence in the gospel. But since I did not want to be baptized until after all my questions were cleared up, I delayed my baptism.

Then one day one of my students in the Foreign Language School said to me, "Recently two young American missionaries have begun boarding at my house."

I asked him, "Will you bring them to the school and introduce them to me?"

The following day he brought the Mormon missionaries to the school and introduced them. As I shook hands with them I felt a very good feeling; their humility especially impressed me very much. They gave me a very courteous invitation, saying: "On the coming Sunday we will hold our first Sunday School in this city at the hall of the Sendai Chamber of Commerce and Industry. Would you please attend our meeting?" I was attracted by their charming invitation. Also I was very surprised when I was told they were "elders," in spite of being so young. My curiosity and good feeling caused me to decide to attend their meeting that Sunday instead of the Methodist Church.

It was the last Sunday of September, 1949, when I attended my first Sunday School meeting of The Church of Jesus Christ of Latter-day Saints. There were only a few people present and the services were very simple, yet I was greatly inspired by the people's sincere hearts. After the meeting two missionaries accompanied me to my house.

Since I had many questions concerning Christianity that had not been answered by either the Catholic father or Protestant ministers, I asked those questions of the two young missionaries. To my surprise they answered clearly and with confidence. They had strong

testimonies about every word in the Bible and also the
Book of Mormon. I was deeply inspired by their strong
faith and meekness, and as they left my house they gave
me a pamphlet, *Joseph Smith Tells His Own Story.*

As I read the booklet I felt so inspired that I couldn't
sleep, so I continued to read until dawn. I was surprised
to learn that the Prophet Joseph Smith saw the living
God, our Heavenly Father, and his Son, Jesus Christ. At
first I couldn't believe it, but something enlightened my
mind and aroused a desire within me to know more
about this incident and to search out facts to see if they
were really true. I started reading the Book of Mormon.
When I found the following scripture in First Nephi my
heart was filled with joy:

"Yea, even my father spake much concerning the
Gentiles, and also concerning the house of Israel, that
they should be compared like unto an olive-tree, whose
branches should be broken off and should be scattered
upon all the face of the earth.

"Wherefore, he said it must needs be that we should
be led with one accord into the land of promise, unto the
fulfilling of the word of the Lord, that we should be
scattered upon all the face of the earth.

"And after the house of Israel should be scattered
they should be gathered together again; or, in time, after
the Gentiles had received the fulness of the Gospel, the
natural branches of the olive-tree, or the remnants of the
house of Israel, should be grafted in, or come to the
knowledge of the true Messiah, their Lord and their
Redeemer." (1 Nephi 10:12-14.)

I was impressed because in those days I had joined
the United Nations Association and had known that the
olive tree is symbolized on the United Nations flag, each
leaf representing a member nation. I found in this
scripture an exact analogy of the United Nations flag. It
seemed to me the goals and purposes for which I had
aimed through participation in the United Nations
Association had become clearer. I gradually realized my
true purpose was here in the Book of Mormon.

Also, when I learned about temple work and about

baptism for the dead and the saving of our ancestors, principles that I couldn't find in any other religion, my joy and gratitude were beyond expression. Many of my relatives and friends had been killed in battle, but now I could be an agent of salvation for them through genealogical work and temple ordinances.

I quit attending the Methodist Church and began to attend the Mormon meetings regularly. The more Mormon doctrine I studied the more my testimony was strengthened. I felt that finally I had found the complete truth I had been seeking for a long time, and I made up my mind to be baptized into the true Church of Jesus Christ.

I was pleased when I heard that a missionary would baptize me in the Hirose River, because it is a custom of Shintoism to cleanse one's whole body in pure water, especially in a river. It was a cold day on November 6, 1949. Brother Lyle Elmer Simonson, who was serving in the army, prepared a truck for us and we all rode to the upper stream of the river, which was flowing between rocks under the mountain.

The water was cold and clean--we could even see fish swimming in its depths. Though I have never been in Israel, I thought of the river Jordan in which the Lord was baptized by the hand of John the Baptist. I was deeply moved when Elder Hugh Lynn Oldham was willing to step into this cold water with me and baptize me by immersion. On the same day at the missionaries' home I was confirmed by Elder Kenji Akagi, and became the firstfruit in Sendai Branch. On Christmas day that year I was ordained a priest.

When the Free Methodist missionary who had been holding Bible classes at my home was informed of my conversion, she stopped at my home one day and gave me a booklet entitled *Mormonism in the Searchlight.* She said to me, "I pray for you that after you read this book, you will return to the right way." I felt very sorry for her, but my strong testimony was never shaken either by this highly critical book or by her admonition.

At the time of my baptism, I had three sons:

Masahisa, nine; Masaji, five; and Masakazu, two. The
following year, on March 26, 1950, my first daughter,
Seiko, was born. On July 4 of that same year I was so
excited to be able to baptize my wife in the same river.
My eldest son, Masahisa, was also baptized that day.
Now that my whole family had become members, we
were the first native Mormon family in the city of
Sendai. Two other brothers and one sister were baptized
on the same day as my wife and son. One brother,
Atsushi Fukuda, later became the first counselor in the
bishopric of the Second Ward, Tokyo Stake. A short
time after his baptism he contracted a lung disease that
put him in the hospital for almost ten years. His disease
became so serious that it was determined that the only
way he could survive would be through a dangerous
operation. His strong faith overcame all hardships. After
the operation his health improved. Now he is working
hard in his company and also in the Church. Whenever
I meet him I am reminded of the words of Paul: ". . . we
glory in tribulations also: knowing that tribulation
worketh patience; And patience, experience; and
experience, hope: And hope maketh not ashamed;
because the love of God is shed abroad in our hearts by
the Holy Ghost which is given unto us." (Romans 5:3-5.)

The sister who was baptized at the same time as
Brother Fukuda, Sister Ryoko Shimada, also became ill
and had to enter the hospital. One day I visited her and
talked with her about the gospel. Later she sent me a
message indicating another woman patient wanted to
hear the gospel from me, so I went with the missionaries
and preached the gospel to her. As I mentioned our
doctrine of anointing with oil, she asked us to anoint her,
so the elders did. She was pleased and with tears told me
the following:

"Since the doctor has said that I will die in the near
future I have been greatly troubled. As I have thought
about my children I have been unable to eat for many
days, but now, thanks to your preaching, I know the
Lord God, and peace has entered into my heart. I have
become completely calm. I am now very happy and it

matters not if I should die or if I can live on."

Her doctor, knowing she would soon die, sent her back home. As she left the hospital she looked back at us and, waving her hand, smiled. I thought of the modern revelation through the Prophet Joseph Smith: "And it shall come to pass that those that die in me shall not taste of death, for it shall be sweet unto them." (D&C 42:46.)

Several days later, I received a letter from her husband informing me that she had died. I visited him and offered flowers at her grave. He told me that when she died she was holding a picture of Jesus Christ, which Sister Shimada had given her, and that he was now reading the Book of Mormon. I told him, "If you and your children are converted into the Church you can do vicarious baptism for her and your family can be sealed together for eternity." He seemed comforted and encouraged.

I baptized my second son, Masaji, on February 2, 1952, the day of his eighth birthday. On April 20 that year I was ordained an elder by Elder Hal G. Ferguson. I was set apart as president of the Sendai Branch on May 13, 1953. My third son, Masakazu, was baptized on the anniversary of the restoration of the Aaronic Priesthood, on May 15, 1955, in the Hirose River. It was a fine spring morning. Clean water was flowing alongside a mountain, which was covered with green trees, grass, and some wild flowers. Birds were singing and seemed to be praising Masakasu's eternal birth. Everything was so beautiful that we imagined we were at the Susquehanna River when John the Baptist appeared to Joseph Smith and Oliver Cowdery on May 15, 1829.

Two daughters were baptized at the Tokyo Mission Home on their eighth birthdays. The day our elder daughter, Seiko, was baptized it was snowing and all nature was covered in white clothing, as if it had prepared a white robe for us.

Our membership increased to more than thirty, and among them was Sister Shio, who was converted from Tenrikyo, a sect of Shintoism. Her family became one of

the most faithful Mormon families in Japan and
provided a strong foundation for the Sendai Branch. I
baptized her on Christmas day, 1951. She first came into
contact with the Church in an interesting way. We used
to hold street meetings in the late afternoon in front of
the Sendai Station, and the missionaries would have
their shoes shined there after street meetings.

Among the shoeshine boys was a war orphan whom
all of the missionaries loved very much. One day he was
bitten by a dog, and the missionaries carried him to a
nearby hospital, where Sister Shio worked. Since her
husband's parents were Tenrikyo preachers, most of her
family was opposed to her conversion and she suffered
much persecution. But her faith was so strong that the
following spring her elder daughter was baptized; then
one by one all her children became members. Finally her
reluctant husband also attended church and, after
several cottage meetings with missionaries, became a
member. He later was called as first counselor of the
district presidency and to other positions.

Brother Shio's father, who had been a preacher of
Tenrikyo, was converted at eighty-four years of age.
Before his conversion, whenever the missionaries visited
Sister Shio's house they saw a sign on the door: "Don't
let missionaries enter here." But this stubborn
father-in-law was finally converted into the Church after
a miraculous healing under the hands of the elders. He
was baptized in the Hirose River a few days after
recovering from his serious sickness.

We fostered many kinds of activities for raising
church building funds, since we didn't have our own
building. Sometimes we held bazaars, selling candy and
clothes, and sometimes we performed concerts or ballets.
We sold ballet tickets on the street and from house to
house.

One day I was attempting to sell tickets in a U.S.
Army residential area, visiting each house. When I
knocked at one house an officer came out and violently
yelled at me: "Who authorized you to sell house to house
in this neighborhood? Don't sell here anymore, and you

must report to the Provost Marshal tomorrow morning at 10 o'clock."

When I went to the office of the Provost Marshal the following morning, he said to me, "I am the Provost Marshal. Now I will judge you. Raise your hand and swear to me to tell only the truth."

As I raised my hand he asked, "Who authorized you to sell such tickets? From whom did you get permission?"

For a while I kept silence, but I prayed in my heart. Then suddenly a voice came out from my mouth: "I was authorized by the Lord Jesus Christ."

After what seemed like a long silence he looked back toward his office staff and said, "At the Sendai Public Hall there is going to be a very nice ballet. If any of you want to go, please raise your hand." Many hands were raised; then he turned to me and said, "Give me ten tickets, and I want to say that I am happy to give you permission to sell the tickets in this American residential area."

I wept and thanked our Lord.

Another time when I was selling fund-raising tickets on the streets in the camp, an American-born Japanese officer passed through and scolded me, ordering me to follow him to his office. There he accusingly inquired, "Why are you selling tickets in this camp?"

"We are raising funds for our own church building," I replied.

"Well, you can't sell the tickets in the camp."

I said, "Many Americans have bought tickets from me. When you were coming to me I thought you also were going to buy. Are you not Japanese? Even foreigners love us Japanese very much. Don't you know that the Japanese people are now miserable materially and spiritually, not knowing the merciful Lord? Can't you see their needs? Are they not your brothers?"

Suddenly a voice behind me said, "Mr. Watabe, give me your tickets. I want to buy."

It was a young girl who had been a student in one of my night school classes. My eyes blurred with tears.

As I learned in the Church that all members are missionaries and each has a responsibility to inform others about the restored gospel, I made up my mind to go tracting every day no matter where I was.

I began tracting in the train on my way to work. One day as I got off the train and was walking along the platform, a student called to me and said, "I overheard your good talk about the gospel in the train from my seat. I would like to hear more about Jesus Christ. Will you teach me?" A few days later he became a member; and about sixteen years later when the Tokyo Stake, the first stake in Japan, was established, he was called to be a member of the high council. Other brothers and sisters have also come into the Church from my tracting on the streets and in trains.

We frequently held street meetings near the crowded train stations. One day as we closed a meeting one earnest investigator stayed and asked us many questions, as if he didn't notice the time passing. It was almost dark when we dismissed the meeting. This investigator soon became a strong member, and later he moved to Tokyo. There he became first counselor in the Tokyo West Branch, and while he was serving in that position he became seriously ill and was taken to the hospital. For two years, while he was confined to the hospital, his faithful wife earned money by selling cosmetics. Among her clients were many who belonged to other religious groups. Some of them said to her, when her husband's sickness became dangerous, "If he would join our church, I am sure he would soon be well."

Hearing this admonition from his wife at his deathbed he said, "I'd rather die as a Mormon than live longer converted to another religion."

Shortly afterwards he died, a true and faithful member of the Church. Just a few days before his death I received his family group sheet record from the Church's Genealogical Department in Salt Lake City, since I was the mission genealogical chairman. As I put the record on my desk I heard a voice say, "Send it to him immediately." So I did. It was in his hand when he died. Later I heard from his wife that he found so much satisfaction in holding his ancestors' record in his hand upon his deathbed that he said, "Now I may go with joy knowing I did something for my ancestors."

Another time I contacted a high school girl on the train and she earnestly listened to my words. She visited our church and our home several times. She thanked me for my instructions about our Savior Jesus Christ, and brought me a young shoot of chrysanthemum and planted it in my garden. At that time she was very busy preparing for a university entrance examination.

About eighteen months later I heard she was in the hospital, so I took some flowers and visited her. To my surprise she confessed that she had tried to commit suicide by taking sleeping pills, because she had failed the entrance examination. Fortunately she had been discovered and saved. I told her that the Church is the greatest of all schools; that the gospel plan is the school of life; that our life on this earth itself is an educational test; and that when we graduate from this school we get a diploma that will take us to our Father's presence. Then I said to her, "Why did you so despair when you failed such a short temporal examination? Please come to church after you recover and become a good student in the school of life."

After she left the hospital she came to church several times and eagerly asked many questions concerning the gospel. But before her conversion could be accomplished, she attempted suicide again. This time her lifeless body wasn't discovered for several days. As I watched her chrysanthemum bush in full flower in my garden, it seemed she was asking me to do vicarious baptism for her.

A few years after I became branch president one of our members was arrested for a criminal offense, and I was summoned to his trial as a witness. When the judge asked me about the brother's character, my heart was filled with love and I bore testimony and witnessed he had been a faithful member, saying, "I think he was caught by Satan just momentarily."

Then I preached the gospel for quite a long time, and to my surprise, while I was talking the people in the courtroom remained silent and earnestly listened to my preaching. I felt the power of the priesthood and remembered the case of the Lord standing before Pilate. Indeed, the Lord was with me while I was preaching before the judge that day.

One day one of the sisters was in a bus accident, and after being anointed with oil, she was soon miraculously healed. Her testimony was strengthened very much by this experience. Later she came to me and asked me to anoint her niece, who was critically ill in the hospital. When we arrived at the hospital, the door to the room where the niece lay was closed and a sign on it said "Visitors Prohibited." But since the mother of the girl and our LDS sister requested so strongly that we be allowed entrance, a doctor finally permitted us to enter and perform an anointing ordinance. When we entered into the room the niece had lost consciousness; her countenence was as pale as death, and she was in an oxygen inhalation unit. We quietly anointed her with the holy oil used by the priesthood to administer to the sick, and I noticed as we were doing so her cheeks gradually reddened, and when we finished the ordinance her consciousness returned. Three days later she left the hospital.

When I was in Sendai, I experienced many times the power of the priesthood. These are some of those sacred experiences:

1. Just a few months after I became a member of the Church the Hirose River flooded, and since my house was on the banks of the river, the water flowed into my house. The missionaries were worried and rushed to my house and helped to carry out all the furniture. When I carried out the books, one missionary cried to me, "Hold up the Book of Mormon! Don't let it get wet!" Indeed, the Book of Mormon has been sacred and valuable for us all our lives.

A few days later the missionaries came to my house to help shovel out the mud. Many of our neighbors were amazed, saying, "Though we have been their enemies and fought against them, now these intelligent young white men are laboring in such mud, in order to help us. What great love they have!"

2. Each member of my family was blessed at various times and healed by the power of the priesthood that I hold. One evening when my eldest son was playing with some fireworks, a firework accidentally exploded in his palm. I rushed to him and noticed all his palm had turned white. Immediately I had him put his palm in some water, then I anointed him. After a few hours his hand was miraculously healed; no skin had peeled off, and after a while there was no scar at all.

3. In those days I was raising chickens and my children were taking care of them. One morning my third son wanted to feed the chickens, and while he was cutting some grass for them the knife slipped and cut his finger to the bone. Quickly I bound it with a bandage and then anointed him, and to my surprise, when I untied the bandage I found that the finger was joined firmly, and after a while even the scar had gone away.

4. One day it was snowing when I baptized a young student in the Hirose River. As I immersed him into the cold water he lost consciousness, but I was so calm and my arm was so strong that I held his body and waded to the bank and after landing we made a fire and had him warmed up. As I shook his body he awoke.

5. An investigator from the Methodist school was visiting our branch; and for a long time after his regular lessons with the missionaries, he didn't want to be baptized, saying, "I believe in the Lord Jesus Christ, but I can't believe Joseph Smith was a prophet." One day I met him in the streetcar and suddenly I began scolding him with a loud voice, saying, "Why can't you believe the Prophet Joseph Smith, while you say you believe the Lord Jesus Christ? If so, you are a hypocrite." After a few days he came to the Church and was baptized. Tears flowed from my eyes when I remembered the following scripture: "Reproving betimes with sharpness, when moved upon by the Holy Ghost; and then showing forth

afterwards an increase of love toward him whom thou
hast reproved, lest he esteem thee to be his enemy."
(D&C 121:43.)

6. One Saturday an investigator came to the church
and asked me to anoint her daughter, because she had
been run over by a bicycle and couldn't stand. She had
been lying in bed for several days. When I went to her
house, I prayed for her with her mother beside the bed.
Early the following Sunday morning the mother came to
the Church, her countenance bright with joy, and told
me her daughter had stood up on her feet immediately
after I left her house and she was walking now. Then she
asked me, "Will you come to see us after sacrament
meeting?" So after sacrament meeting I went to the
home. As I entered the house the daughter came back
from a neighbor's house and told me, "Look--my foot!
It was healed completely and now I am playing with my
friend."

7. One Sunday after Sunday School a missionary
was suddenly caught by an evil spirit and began to act
violently. We took him upstairs to the missionaries'
room, and while two missionaries held him, I, as branch
president, anointed him; immediately he became quiet
and slept. Just before sacrament meeting he awoke and
came down to attend the meeting. Since it was the first
Sunday of the month, we held a testimony meeting. He
bore his testimony as follows: "While I was receiving the
blessing an evil spirit came out from my body, and I felt
the power of the priesthood, and peace entered my
heart. Then I feel asleep, and now I am refreshed
completely."

8. In our country the primary schools offer lunch to
the children. Since they were putting coffee in milk, my
daughter didn't drink it. Then one day the teacher
noticed and asked my daughter, who was in the first
grade at that time, why. My daughter answered that it
was because she believed in the Word of Wisdom. The
teachers discussed the matter among themselves and
finally decided not to put coffee into the milk anymore.

Another time my daughter's class members wanted

to give their teacher something on his birthday, and
since he liked tobacco they decided to present a cigarette
case. But my daughter told them about the Word of
Wisdom: "If you buy a cigarette case, I can't join you. I
will buy something else that is good for him, and present
it to him by myself." The class committee consulted and
finally decided to buy something else.

When I was working at the Japanese Foreign Office
in Sendai, after I became a member of the Church I quit
attending their parties, because it is a Japanese custom
to pour wine for each other and drink toasts at parties.
When our office invited others as guests it was a required
courtesy for the host to pour wine into others' cups. I was
warned several times by my superior, "You must attend
these parties—this is a part of your job."

I was also warned to stop participating in the
missionary street meetings. "A government officer should
not become involved in such activity," I was told. But I
continued to attend the street meetings and, of course, I
refused to attend the parties.

Then one day my superior called me and said, "You
would rather go to your church and work there; we don't
need you anymore." Thus I was discharged from the
Foreign Office. But the Lord was watching over me, and
after a while, LDS Chaplain Nelson, a member of the
Church, found me a job in the U.S. Army camp. I
worked for five years for the Occupation Forces, and
when the camp was closed I was called to the mission
home to work as a translator for the Church. My family
and I moved to the Tokyo area (my residence is
Yokohama) in August 1957. That December I was set
apart as first counselor in the Tokyo Branch presidency.
The following year I was ordained mission genealogical
chairman, and I served in that position until March 15,
1970, when the Tokyo Stake was organized. I also served
at various times as district high councilor and as first
counselor in the district presidency.

During the period when I was a mission genealogical
chairman, in the summers of 1965, 1967, and 1969,
excursions to the Hawaii Temple were sponsored. We

were blessed to attend the first and second of those excursions, and on July 23, 1965, my wife and I were sealed for eternity in the Hawaiian Temple. The following day my eldest son, Masahisa, who was on the way back to graduate school at Brigham Young University after a two-year mission in Japan, stopped over in Hawaii and was sealed to us. He had entered Utah State University in the summer of 1960. After one year of study at Utah State University, he transferred to BYU. When he was in graduate school at BYU in 1965 he married Faith Okawa of Hawaii, who also attended BYU and who also had served a mission to Japan.

In the summer of 1962 my second son, Masaji, also went to BYU. After his sophomore year he also was called on a mission to his homeland.

Both Masahisa and Masaji, in the later part of their missions, were assigned to be branch presidents. It was a great thrill and wonderful experience that I was a district councilor visiting their branches and could see their work as branch presidents.

Masaji had graduated from high school in Yokohama, and when he departed from the port of Yokohama for the United States, more than one hundred classmates came to the harbor to see him off. They surrounded him, sang songs, and clapped their hands. A cheer went up, and they then presented him with a traditional Japanese bouquet.

In the summer of 1966 Masaji finished his mission in Japan and went back to BYU, where he completed his junior and senior years and then finished a two-year master's degree. After this he was assigned to the Church College of Hawaii as an assistant professor of mathematics.

In the summer of 1966 my third son, Masakazu, went to BYU. After he finished his sophomore year, he was called on a mission to Brazil. When he received his mission call, at first he was discouraged, since he wanted to come to Japan and work in his own nation. But later he enjoyed his work in Brazil, especially among the Japanese, and he contributed to the establishment of a

Japanese branch there. He helped convert several
Japanese families. It was marvelous in the Lord's work
that one of his converts, Tatsui Sato, was a man whom I
first contacted many years before in a streetcar in
Sendai.

When I was the Sendai Branch president, it was my
regret that when the missionary organist moved out,
there often was no organist in the branch. Therefore,
when my daughters were born I was determined that as
they grew up I would like to have them learn the piano
so they could become organists in the Church. God
blessed us greatly and my desire was granted. Both of
them became organists in the Yokohama Ward of the
Tokyo Stake. Yasuko played for Sunday School and for
MIA, and Seiko played for sacrament meetings. Seiko
was also the first counselor of the YWMIA and taught
the Laurel class. She also taught kindergarten. My last
and fourth son, Masasue, has also been active in the
Church and in his priesthood quorums.

In the Yokohama Branch, my wife, Hisako, served as
a Relief Society president for three years, then second
counselor of the Relief Society district presidency. When
the branch became a ward I was ordained a seventy, and
in order to help me with my proselyting work she asked
to be released from her office. We enjoyed teaching
investigators and having cottage meetings with them in
our home.

From 1964 to 1966 we enjoyed building our own
church building. It was a wonderful project. All of our
family joined in this program and had many new
experiences that we never had before. During this time
two brothers who were engaged in the construction were
severely wounded when they fell about sixteen feet to a
concrete floor. Brother Okamoto broke his arm and his
upper and lower jaws. When we took him to the hospital
the doctor said he could live only a few hours. Brother
Asama had broken his spine.

The branch president and I administered to them,
called an ambulance, and took them to a larger hospital.
The doctor of this larger hospital gave them the same

sentence. But since they had poured out their precious blood for the work of the Lord, the Lord himself blessed them and they were miraculously healed within a month. Later Brother Okamoto became one of the outstanding members of the Tokyo Stake high council, and Brother Asama became the first bishop of Yokohama Ward. In the spring of 1967, when Elder Hugh B. Brown of the Council of the Twelve came to Yokohama and dedicated the building as the Lord's house, all members who labored for this sacred building wept for joy.

In 1954, when we were in the Sendai Branch, the members bought a building to serve as our chapel, and Elder Harold B. Lee came to dedicate it. It was a great honor when he asked me to be his interpreter. I still remember the experience as if it were yesterday. When I stood by him and while I was doing interpreting he was embracing me and I felt as if I were in a huge rock. At that time, a district conference was also held in Sendai. In the morning session my daughter Seiko, only four years old, gave the opening prayer on the stage. Elder Lee called me to the podium to do interpreting for her, and then Seiko and I sat next to Sister Lee. Since the morning session would continue for two hours, I worried if Seiko could keep quiet to the end. My worry became reality when she began to move. To my surprise, Sister Lee took a piece of candy from her handbag and gave it to Seiko so she would keep quiet until she ate it up. And when she started to move again, Sister Lee again gave her another piece. She repeated this three or four times. Then finally she took out a pencil and paper and gave it to her. My daughter started drawing a doll on the paper, and thanks to Sister Lee's great love, she kept quiet on the stage until the end of the meeting.

In the afternoon we had a testimony meeting, and three of my boys one by one stood before the congregation and bore strong testimony. As I attended the servicemen's sacrament meeting in the evening, Elder Lee mentioned my daughter's prayer and sons' testimonies in his talk, saying they were inspired by the

Holy Ghost; otherwise they couldn't have prayed or
borne testimony at such a young age. The next morning
when I went with Elder and Sister Lee to the station,
Sister Lee took a piece of paper from her handbag and
showed it to me, saying, "This is what your daughter
drew. I will keep it as a token of our trip to Japan." I
kept back my tears with difficulty, and thanked her for
her great love.

Time is an arrow. Fourteen years later, when little
Seiko was eighteen years old, my family was sealed
together for eternity by Elder Lee in the Salt Lake
Temple.

Since I was baptized it had been my greatest dream
that all my family could be sealed in the temple, and
part of this dream was realized when we participated in
the first temple excursion to the Hawaii Temple in the
summer of 1965, when Masahisa joined us and was
sealed to us. The rest of my children weren't sealed then,
but the Lord blessed us so much that we could all be
sealed in the Salt Lake Temple. On August 9, 1968, with
Elder Lee officiating, our longtime dream was realized
completely. It was the best day in all our life.

20

MASAKAZU WATABE: THE SECOND GENERATION

My name is Masakazu Watabe. I was born in
Sendai, in the northern part of Japan, on May 11, 1947.
When I was two years old my father joined the Church,
and after his conversion, from what I have heard, my
mother and older brothers were impressed with the
changes that came into his life. I was baptized on May
15, 1955, when I was eight years old, in the Hirose River.
I remember that day well. I was baptized by my father,
who was president of the Sendai Branch, and I
remember my father asking me about the truthfulness of
the Church. I also remember answering yes, I do know
that the Church is true. However, I really wasn't sure at
that age. But I do recall the good feeling I had.

I was practically raised in the Church, so as a boy it
seemed to me that Church life, the way I lived, was the
life of all Japanese. Probably my first realization that I
might be different from other Japanese people occurred
when an American in Sendai came to our house. We
lived near the elementary school, and I was in about
second or third grade at that time. This man was one of
the few Americans who had ever come to that area. He

couldn't speak Japanese, of course, so my dad talked to him in English. The American was eating Japanese noodles with chopsticks, and that seemed to attract the other children in the elementary school, who came over to watch him. I was very embarrassed because everybody in town seemed to be talking behind my back, saying, "That little Masakazu knows a Caucasian." My first reaction was embarrassment, but I was used to seeing American missionaries at church, so it didn't seem to be so strange that we would have an American at home. That was my first realization of being different from all other Japanese kids my own age.

I loved the Church, not because I was fed spiritually in the meetings, but because the meetinghouse had a very nice backyard with all kinds of trees, and we used to pick fruit there. Also, I loved my associations with the children at church.

The members in that branch were very kind. I still remember some of the Primary and Junior Sunday School teachers. But going to church was quite a task, because we had to take a train for about thirty minutes. Sometimes my father had to go to the church very early in the morning, so my brother and I had to ride the train alone. After getting off at the station we had to walk about twenty minutes.

We moved to Yokohama when I was in fourth grade. Yokohama had a branch president who was a missionary, but shortly after we moved there, Shozo Suzuki, who later became patriarch of the Osaka Stake, was called to serve as the branch president, and my father became one of his counselors. In Yokohama we had to walk twenty or thirty minutes to the station, then take an electric train for about ten minutes to another station, and walk a short distance to church. I made friends in the Yokohama Branch, and the association with those friends was very important to me. I began to really realize that I was different from other Japanese friends because I was a Mormon. For example, in the city there was more social life. Whenever I was invited to a birthday party they always served Japanese tea or coffee, and I couldn't take those things, whereas others could. That really made me realize that I was quite different from the other children.

About the time I was in junior high school I became keenly self-conscious of differences between me and other students in the school. I was proud of being a member of the Church, and I really wanted to do missionary work, to talk my friends into attending church with me. In fact, I am pleased to say that one of them finally joined the Church.

One of my teachers in junior high school really inspired me. We used to read many novels—not only Japanese but also Western. Sometimes I read Shakespeare's works in translation. This teacher used to ask, "Now, what is the author trying to say?" He always came up with some moral teaching in the class. He also introduced Confucianism and other philosophies of Japan and China. His teaching matched just right with the teachings I received in church and at home. I used to go to his office to talk with him. He knew that I was a Christian. In fact, he encouraged me to become a preacher or minister. He didn't know that in the Mormon Church we don't have paid ministers.

I was aware by then of some Church teachings, and I really enjoyed the religious and spiritual part of the Church—not necessarily of Mormonism, but of Christianity. At that time I started to read the Bible. It seemed to me the answer to all the problems of the world. How Christ lived, not only what he taught in parables, but what he himself did, was very attractive to me. I read the Bible in Japanese. Even though I was attending Sunday School classes and priesthood classes, I never read other standard works as a youth. But I read the New Testament and enjoyed it very much.

In high school, conflict had started in my life. My teachers were much more cynical and secular. Some teachers were brilliant—graduates of good universities in Japan. I remember one teacher who asked, "Now is there anybody who still believes in fable stories such as in the Christian Bible—superstitions such as God, and so

forth?" I didn't raise my hand to defend the Church. On
the contrary, the question started me thinking whether
what I believed and what I had been taught was true. I
started doubting the existence of God even though I
believed in the teachings of the Church and in the Bible.
I began wondering whether Joseph Smith really saw
God and Jesus Christ, as I had been taught. I prayed to
the Lord, saying, "Well, if Joseph Smith saw God, why
can't I see God also?" That was my situation when
Brother Kenji Tanaka became our branch president. I
really thank Heavenly Father for having sent him as my
branch president at the time because I believe if it
hadn't been for him and some other faithful members of
the Yokohama Branch who influenced me, I probably
wouldn't be active in the Church today.

One Sunday morning in priesthood class Brother
Tanaka asked, "Is there anybody here who really doubts
the existence of God?" That was at the very time when I
did. He said, "If there is, I would like to give you a
challenge. Every night before you go to bed, please go
outside and look at the stars for at least five or ten
minutes. Be sure to do that every day."

When I went out the first few days, there wasn't any
change at all. But soon I found myself praying to
Heavenly Father on my knees and really talking to him,
and that gave me a testimony.

In 1963 I was working as a houseboy for the
American missionaries at the Yokohama Branch. I
cleaned, cooked, and helped with the laundry. We lived
in an apartment in the branch meetinghouse. After a
meeting one night a missionary sister's purse was stolen.
In it were her passport, dictionary, and money.

We looked for it but couldn't find it anywhere. Then
we called the police, and they investigated. After a while
almost everybody had gone home. A friend was coming
over to the chapel to stay with us that night, so I went
outside to unlock the door for him. As I was returning I
met one of the foreign missionaries. When he saw me he
suggested, "Maybe we ought to look around in the shrubs
in front of the chapel. Would you mind going with me?"

I said, "Okay, let's go." As we were going outside to
the park we found the stolen purse right in front of the
church, by the gate, so we called the police again.
Everything was still in the purse except the money.

The policeman said, "This is really strange. It must
have been taken by someone who knows the area really
well, an inside job; and it must have been somebody
who is very young, because a more experienced thief
wouldn't do it this way. It must have been some young
kid who got scared and threw it here in haste—someone
in high school, probably." The policeman's implication
was clear to me. Suddenly I felt that everybody was
looking at me. That really struck me hard. Here I was—I
had been raised in the Church, I had been taught all
these teachings, and now what a shame! (To the
Japanese, shame is something really, really terrible.) I
felt that everybody was accusing me, especially the
missionary who had seen me coming in and thought that
I returned the purse and was coming back to the house. I
suffered greatly; in fact, I couldn't sleep, and I prayed
constantly, saying, "Lord, I know that you are there, and
I know that you are on the side of righteous people. Also
I know that I am innocent. You know that I am
innocent. I know that you will help me—that you will
save me and will show the world that I am innocent." I
don't know whether this feeling was so strong because I
am Japanese and didn't want to shame the Watabe
family among the Church members, but I felt great
shame. And I wanted to see the thief caught and
punished.

I prayed that whole night that the Lord would
expose the real thief to the world. By doing so, he could
show the world that I was innocent, that I didn't do
things like that.

The next morning I was so depressed that I couldn't
get out of bed to go to school. I fasted, and I really
believed that if I did everything possible the Lord would
answer my prayer. That night I had to get up and cook
for the missionaries. And after dinner, after all the
missionaries had gone, I was still praying in my mind

when Brother Tanaka came in. He had been released as branch president about two weeks before that, and he entered now with the new branch president. When I saw him I could not hold it any longer. I just broke down and cried and cried. I told him what had happened and how I felt. I asked him why the Lord hadn't answered my prayers. As he listened, he was also in tears.

He said something like this: "Do you think you prayed right? Do you think Christ would have prayed as you did? If it were Christ, do you think he would have prayed to show the world that he was innocent? Remember what Christ went through and what he taught. On the cross, even though he was innocent, he said, 'Father, forgive them, for they know not what they do.' Now, compared to his prayer, do you think your prayer was right? If you were really a Christian, wouldn't you pray to the Father to forgive this thief, or ask him to help this person not to do anything like that again, instead of trying to show your innocence or see him punished?"

That really touched my heart. Suddenly I really realized what the teachings of Christ should mean to us. Until then I had had a testimony, but I didn't really understand how hard it is to live the gospel or what the real meaning of Christ's atonement is. I went alone into my room and prayed again. Then I felt a wonderful peace.

A few days later, Brother Tanaka said, "I think we know who the thief is." The thief, who had been at the chapel that night, had also tried to break into the branch president's office.

Well, that was a great experience. It shows what the gospel can do for people, any time, any place.

My two older brothers were in the United States at that time, and I was trying to decide where to attend college after I graduated from high school. In the minds of some Japanese Latter-day Saints, academic standards of U.S. colleges are not as high as those of the better schools in Japan. Generally, the best young people in the Church qualified to enroll in a Japanese university.

There are important advantages socially and
professionally in attending a Japanese university rather
than going to a foreign school. Some Japanese people are
very prejudiced, not only in secular society but also in
the Church. There is an attitude that the best students
attend only the best universities in Japan.

Because of this feeling, I really wanted to go to a
respectable Japanese university. My eldest brother had
attended a Japanese university, but since he studied
English it was reasonable that he would go to the States
to further his education. My father encouraged us to go
to BYU. "It's the Lord's school, so it's the best school,"
he would say. My second brother was one of the smartest
students in the prefecture of Kanagawa. He received a
scholarship that placed him ninth place among all
students. But among the top forty high school scholars of
the prefecture, all except Masaji were accepted at Tokyo
University, the school of greatest prestige. He had been
majoring in science, and Tokyo University had the most
distinguished program in the country, but somehow
Masaji failed his entrance examination.

Only about 30 percent of the high school students
who enter Tokyo University go directly from high
school; another 70 percent go to a preparatory school to
prepare for passing the exams. Thus, when Masaji failed,
he wanted to go to preparatory school and try again the
next year. Our father told him that he ought to go to
BYU, which was the best school in the whole world,
because that is the Lord's university, and that all these
secular considerations of going to Tokyo University
weren't important. I remember the big argument over
this issue at home. Masaji didn't have a Brother Tanaka
at the time he needed one in his life, as I did. His secular
teachers really influenced him greatly, although he
attended his church meetings. At any rate, my father
won the argument, and Masaji left Japan and went to
BYU.

After seeing all this at home, I was determined to
attend a Japanese university. I felt that even though a
person is active in the Church and has strong faith, he

doesn't have to sacrifice knowledge and the other secular blessings of Japan. I felt I could be active in the Church and still attend a Japanese university.

One thing that really influenced me at that time and place was meeting Brother Spencer Palmer and a missionary named John Chase, both of whom encouraged me to attend BYU. Brother Palmer gave me counsel that as a true Latter-day Saint I should seek to excel in all things, including the secular world. He challenged me to find a field in which I could excel. So I said that if I failed the Japanese university exams I would probably apply at BYU.

I decided to enter Tokyo Kyoiku University, one of Japan's best teacher-training schools, to study agricultural economics. But I still had my dilemma, because I had promised Brother Chase and Brother Palmer I would go to BYU. I took the entrance examination and was accepted by Tokyo Kyoiku University with a full scholarship. If I went to BYU it would be terribly expensive, and our family didn't have any money; yet my father kept insisting that BYU is the Lord's school. Something he said really touched me: "Son, you are not really my son. Your mother and I just borrowed you from Heavenly Father for a short time with responsibility to raise you up until you can wisely make your own decisions. You have reached that time of life. Now instead of asking me, go ask your Heavenly Father what you should do." I followed his counsel and received an answer. I decided to go to BYU.

Before I continue, I'd like to talk a little bit about my feelings toward the United States. When I was young and still in Japan, my friends asked me many times, "You're a Mormon? You really belong to an American church?" I resented those questions. I used to say, "It's not an American church. It's the Church of Jesus Christ and it's not an American religion at all." I always resented being identified as American—not only with Americans, but with America. Even though I liked the missionaries, some of the American servicemen in Japan had led corrupt lives and I didn't want to be identified with such evils. Another reason is that most Japanese people sympathize with those who are the underdogs or the losers in life. During the time of the Vietnam war many Japanese people sympathized with the little country of Vietnam, which was fighting against the United States, such a big nation. This may help explain why I felt reluctant to be associated with the States or with America.

I arrived in the United States on April 21, 1966. I planned to go to BYU for two years and then go back to a Japanese university. But after I arrived at BYU, my life, and of course many of my attitudes, were completely changed. Being in a BYU ward also changed me.

When I started attending church activities in the United States I couldn't dance, so I took a dance class. And I learned to love it! Such things as going to a football game and starting it with prayer really impressed me. Social and spiritual things blended beautifully, and they didn't seem to blend that well back in Japan. As I reflect upon things I do with Mormon people in America, it seems quite different from Church life in Japan. In Provo nearly everyone is a member of the Church, and I really enjoy it. I have a new kind of home feeling here. I was reared as a Mormon and came to live in a Mormon community. Once when seven Japanese governors visited BYU, one of them said, "We thank all you faculty members and advisers for letting some of our countrymen stay with you here in this wonderful school." I thought, why is he claiming us as a part of him? These are my people. He's the outsider, and I am a part of the worldwide Mormon family.

There was only one exception to this. Once I dated a girl whose parents were very much against the idea of interracial marriage. Well, I didn't have any intention of marrying her or anything but just going out, but her parents worried. They treated me very coldly. That's the only time that I really felt like an outsider among the members in Utah.

Something else that really turned me off was when

someone would come out and say that the United States
is the best and most blessed country of all the world.
That really bothered me. I felt like, "Wait just a minute!
That's exactly what the Japanese people used to say
about Japan before the war." They used to say that
Japan was the best country—that God would never
forsake Japan and no one could overcome Japan. But
that wasn't so. So it seems that this kind of patriotism
and nationalism rarely serves good spiritual or moral
ends.

May I make just one comment on the chosen race.
The Japanese have taught that they are a specially
chosen or different race from the Caucasians. But does
that really make any difference? As I read the scriptures,
and especially the teachings of the Book of Mormon, I
can't believe that one race is chosen and others, by
nature or heritage, are not. The important thing is
whether one is a faithful member of the Church. I
wouldn't mind being inferior as long as I can live as
Christ did; that is the most important thing.

I have faith in only one church, whose members
come from many different cultures. In fact, I might be
thought of as the product of a tricultural heritage. I am
a young Japanese who has been educated in America
and who was called on a mission to Brazil. I speak
Japanese, English, and Portuguese. In fact, I worked for
a time in the Language Training Mission in Provo
teaching Portuguese to newly called missionaries. I love
Brazil and the South American people, and I have a
deep affection for their literature. As human beings we
can't help but see the world in bits and pieces; we can't
help but be imperfect and incomplete, as we strive
toward perfection and completeness. To Heavenly
Father, all his children and the whole world are before
him at the same time, and he sees the total picture.

After my mission I spent one semester at BYU again;
then I returned to Japan for summer vacation. I had
been away for four years, and I felt that I should be
marrying a Japanese girl. So did my family. I hadn't met
anyone special at BYU, but in Japan it was also difficult,

because now I was accustomed to American ways. I began introducing myself to several of the young sisters, not really remembering that it was a traditional sin to go out with several girls before marriage. Japanese custom does not allow free selection or dating.

I received all kinds of criticism from my family as well as from others in the Church. Here I was, a returned missionary, thrilled to be back and bearing testimony, but there was talk that "he dates many girls--one after another. That's not really good."

By the end of the summer I had become acquainted with one nice girl, whom my family really liked. She was an active member of the Church, and I thought for a while that we might get married. My family was very anxious that we should. But it became very clear to me that marriage is not an arrangement rooted in traditions or based on a family's social position, but a contract between two worthy members of the Church, a man and a woman in love--in love with each other and in love with the Lord. I came to realize more than before that marriage is an eternal, religious contract, not a social arrangement.

That summer in Japan brought into focus some conflicts between Japanese traditions and the principles of the restored gospel, and renewed conviction that a happy marriage must be ordained of God and that for a true Latter-day Saint, marriage must take place in the temple. I concluded that no other satisfaction-- economic or political advantage or family and social approval included--could compare with the personal satisfaction of strictly adhering to the will of the Lord.

When I returned to BYU at the end of the summer I was convinced of three things: (1) that it was not immoral to look around before marriage, (2) that it wasn't required that a native boy from Japan marry a native Japanese girl, and (3) that I would receive a spiritual witness from the Lord as to whom I should marry. I would seek the right person instead of the right language, culture, or color.

That year I came in contact with Rose Nakata,

whom I had known in Brazil, where she had served in
the Brazil Central Mission with headquarters in Sao
Paulo. I was very impressed with her as a missionary
because she was so diligent and faithful. In retrospect,
the very first time I met her there was a special feeling.
But I didn't tell anyone, and after that I completely
forgot about it. I had not thought of her as a dating
candidate. Now I saw her on campus and decided we
should do things together.

Rose is of Japanese ancestry, *sansei* (a
third-generation Japanese-American) from Hawaii, born
on the island of Maui. Her mother is second-generation
Japanese, and her father is third-generation.

Rose does not speak Japanese fluently, but she can
understand some because her mother had lived in Japan
for many years and talked to her at home in Japanese.
Notwithstanding this, Rose is a very "Japanesey"
person.

The bond between us was strengthened by the gospel
and our activity together in the Church, so we were
married in the Hawaii Temple on August 24, 1973.

I am now* attending the University of Southern
California, studying linguistics, and trying to finish my
Ph.D. degree. I have received a special USC fellowship,
and I teach both Japanese classes to American students
and English classes to foreign students. I've already
traveled far since my childhood days as a young
Mormon boy in Sendai, and I have been greatly blessed
through membership in the Church.

---

*This interview was conducted in 1974.

21
FAITH OKAWA WATABE: AN AMERICAN-BORN JAPANESE

I guess the thing that characterizes my life is that I have never belonged to the major portion of the group within which I live. This is true at present and it was true in the past. This is partly because of my cultural background and partly because of my religion. My background in the Church begins with my father, who joined the Church when he was ten years old. His name is Hisashi Okawa, and his father and mother were from the same village on the island of Kyushu in Japan. His father (my grandfather), as a boy of nineteen, was required to seek his fortune elsewhere than in his homeland because he was the second son, and therefore had no inheritance. All of the family property had been promised to the eldest son.

It is said that the reason there are so many *nisei* and *sansei* in the United States from areas like Yamaguchi, Kumamoto (which is where my grandfather and mother are from), and Hiroshima is that the people in those areas live close to the ocean. I guess it is characteristic of all peoples that have ever lived close to the ocean to want to cross it. So when he was urged to seek his

fortune in foreign lands, it wasn't difficult for my
grandfather to decide to take a job with an American
company that was contracting Japanese workers for a
sugar plantation in Hawaii. He was contracted
originally for a three-year period, and after recontracting
a few times he realized that he wasn't ever going back to
Japan.

My grandfather's name is Ichihei Okawa. He and his
brothers eventually ended up in Hawaii and they all
sent for picture brides, girls from their own village. My
grandmother, whose name was Sue Miyata, was really a
picture bride for another man. He was an elderly man
who had never been married, and he died shortly after
their marriage, when she was expecting her first child.
Everybody said, "Poor girl, so far away from home, and
a widow, and expecting!" So they encouraged my
grandfather, who had not contracted for a bride, to
marry her. He was nearly thirty. He agreed because she
was a girl from his own village, and so they were
married.

My father, who was the second child in their family
of eight, was born on the island of Oahu in the town of
Laie. This was very good fortune for us since that is
where the Church decided to have its headquarters
when it first opened up Church work in Hawaii.

Father was born in 1907. He was present at the
dedication of the Hawaii Temple in 1919, and as a
young boy he was pictured on the photograph that was
displayed in the temple. They lived just behind where
the temple is presently located.

When my father grew up, the Church influence was
all around him. He attended a mission school taught by
sister missionaries. The influence of the missionaries on
the family was great, but for some reason, my father was
the only one in his family ever to be baptized.
Apparently the missionaries had been after the family to
let the children be baptized from the time they were all
little children. They all attended Primary. When my
father was ten years old, the Primary planned an outing,
and in order to go on the outing, each child had to have

his parent's signature in case there was an accident. The
missionaries brought the permission for baptism along
also and said, "Sign here and here," and my grandfather
put his "X" in both places. He thought he was just
giving permission for the boy to go on a picnic. Father
came home all wet, which wasn't unusual for him;
Grandfather just thought he had gone to the beach. This
is how my father was baptized.

At first, when my grandfather found out what had
happened, he was upset. He belonged to the Buddhist
religion, and when he left Japan his father said, "You
may never come home to Japan but there is one thing I
would like you to never do, and that is to forsake your
religion." Once my grandfather was ready to be
baptized into the Mormon Church, but my
grandmother reminded him of that promise. So from
that time on he firmly refused to consider it again. The
family was very pleased, when my grandmother died in
1968, that he requested that her funeral be in the
Church. We were surprised because nearly all the
relatives in the family who had passed away up until
then had all been cared for in Buddhist ceremonies. But
he requested a Mormon funeral, so we assume that if he
does not have a testimony of the Church he at least has a
lot of admiration for it and a very dear feeling where it is
concerned.

The mission school that my father attended was only
a grade school, so when he completed the grades there he
had to move away from home and rent a room in
Honolulu. He was able to go home only once or twice a
year. At this time he lost track of the Church and the
Church lost track of him, so he was inactive from the
time he was a young boy in the Aaronic Priesthood. He
graduated from high school, and then normal school,
and was given a contract to teach on the junior high
school level on the island of Maui. It was there that he
met my mother. She had graduated from the University
of Hawaii in home economics and was a home extension
agent for the University of Maui.

Mother was born in Hilo on the island of Hawaii

and, different from my father's humble beginnings, her father was somewhat of a philanthropist. He owned a drugstore business but spent very little time working at it. His wife did all the work and he spent his time in philanthropic activities. Mother was the only daughter in a family of five children, and her childhood was more like that of the Japanese than of the American-Japanese. She was American because of citizenship, but her parents still had very close ties with Japan. Their home was special in the neighborhood. They had in their home tatami mats and other Japanese furnishings that were imported at great expense. She was trained in many of the social amenities that nice young Japanese girls are trained in, such as tea ceremonies and Japanese dance.

Mother spoke only Japanese for the first five or six years of her life, so English is her second language. She had to attend an American public school, but afterwards she went to the Buddhist temple, where she attended Japanese school classes. She did this for all twelve years of her schooling, so she can read and write and is very fluent in spoken Japanese.

My mother's family name, Machida, is still well-known in Hilo. The family owns a large wholesale drugstore business, and her brothers are still running it. As the only daughter in the family, she had been pampered. After she finished high school, she wanted to go to college, to the University of Hawaii. Her mother was opposed to it, for traditional Japanese people prefer that girls not be well educated—it makes them poor wives and mothers. But her mother finally agreed on the condition that she take up some womanly subject. So she graduated in home economics education as a dietitian.

After graduation she still wasn't ready for marriage. She had been introduced by a matchmaker a number of times through the years, and it was only proper that she be married at the proper age, but she just wasn't ready. She was finally married at twenty-seven.

She met my father on Maui at a social sponsored by the Congregational Church. They were both active in that church, though only my mother was a member. By that time my father had completely moved away from the influence of the Mormons. They courted for two years, and my mother's brothers were opposed to her marrying him, since he was just a struggling schoolteacher. But finally they were married, and their first four children were born in Maui. I was the third in the family.

Pearl Harbor was bombed on December 7, 1941, and I was born six days later, on the thirteenth, during a blitz. That night a ship had shot cannon balls onto the beach on Maui. Because of the war, most of the teachers during the war were poorly paid, for the government was expending all of its money on the war. So my father suffered a great cut in salary. Because he wasn't able to support his family anymore on his salary, he did odd jobs, such as printing. When his younger brother suggested that he move back to Honolulu and open up a grocery store business next to the brother's restaurant on the main road in Waikiki, my father thought this might be an opportunity to start a new line of work, so he moved the family to Manoa, on the island of Oahu.

When the war ended all of the store's servicemen patrons went home and my father's business crumbled. He bought a ten-acre farm in the country and thought he would just farm for a little while, but it didn't pay off, so he went back to teaching.

My father returned to activity in the Church through the missionaries. My parents had been married fourteen years then, and there had been only one time during those fourteen years when my mother gave a little thought to the LDS Church. When we were living in Maui, one day two Mormon missionaries came to the house tracting. At that time she didn't bother to tell them her husband was a Mormon, although she was aware of it. And she didn't bother to mention the missionary visit to him. But she recalls that after she turned them away, as she looked out the kitchen window and watched them going away across the field, a terrible feeling came over her that she had done something really wrong. She felt lonely and insecure. But then she was taken up again in her busy life and she forgot about it.

When we moved to Oahu and my father was running his business in Waikiki, about the second or third year that we were there, the missionaries came again, this time looking purposely for my father because he was an inactive member of the Aaronic Priesthood. From then on my mother began investigating the Church. She studied with the elders for a long time and was baptized in 1949. My two eldest sisters, who were then over eight years of age, were also baptized. When Mother was baptized she was asked to bear her testimony. I remember that was the first time I had ever seen her cry and I was really surprised. Since that day our family has been active in the Church. My father returned to activity and about a year later he was made an elder, and we all went to the temple to be sealed.

Our farm was in the country, and we had to travel over seven miles to school and about five miles to church. In the whole branch we were the only Japanese family. There may also have been a few part-Chinese members, but primarily the members were Hawaiians.

All the time I was in high school, or maybe even after I graduated from high school, I had looked down on the Hawaiians. I realize now that I did. I considered us the more superior race. I was a racist without even realizing it. The school we attended was in a different district than the people with whom we attended church. Most of my good friends were Japanese and there wasn't a single other person in my class who was a member of the Church. I was quite apologetic about not belonging to one of the Protestant churches, as all my friends did, although at the same time I was quite fiery about The Church of Jesus Christ of Latter-day Saints being the only true church. My whole life was like that--always being in conflict with the mainstream, the group around me.

Early in my church life I sometimes had callings to teach classes of children my age or older. I was the teacher because I read the best. I was blessed in being able to take seminary for a while from a serviceman's wife, Sister Deon Wall, but we only had seminary until her husband was transferred. That was the beginning of my real interest in studying the scriptures seriously. But even then we only studied the Old Testament. Nobody ever challenged me to read the Book of Mormon. I had no idea what was in the Book of Mormon until I attended Church College of Hawaii. When I read the Book of Mormon in my Book of Mormon class I was fascinated. I thought it seemed to be a continuation of the Old Testament.

When I was in the tenth grade my father was called to be the manager of the Church welfare farm in Laie. He hadn't had much time to farm, so he was happy for the chance to move. He was also happy to be moving back to his home town, to Laie, where he was born. This was the beginning of the real development of my testimony. In Laie the Church was central in all the people's lives. There were lots of young members—children of teachers at the Church College of Hawaii. I found that I was much more comfortable in their company than any other company before, even though most of them were Caucasians. When I completed high school in Laie, I decided to go to Church College of Hawaii instead of the University of Hawaii, where all my friends were planning to go. This was the most important period in my life, as far as the growth of my knowledge of Church doctrine and my testimony of it was concerned.

When I was a sophomore and was taking a Book of Mormon class, our teacher challenged us to apply Moroni 10:4-5 in our lives. I remember kneeling and praying one night; I had read King Benjamin's speech also, and the truth of these scriptures really struck me that night. I was not able to go to sleep, so I got up again, turned the lamp on again, and reread those verses. I suppose if there was any time I was really spiritually moved, that was the very first time of my entire life. It was brief, but I felt as if a light had started to glimmer within. So after graduating from Church

College of Hawaii, I decided to complete my schooling
at Brigham Young University.

We had always been taught to marry in the Church
and my father had told us that we should marry
Japanese. He said, "If you marry a good man, I'll
probably get used to him. But I would be happier if you
would marry a Japanese boy." Most Japanese in Hawaii
usually marry within the race. I hadn't dated much in
high school or college—just a few school dances and
parties. I had gone out with one young man who was
Hawaiian-Caucasian, but my mother wasn't very happy
about that.

At BYU I met Masahisa Watabe. I had declared
rather vehemently to one of my professors at Church
College of Hawaii that I would never consider marrying
a Japanese from Japan. To me, a Japanese from Japan
was just as foreign as any of the non-Japanese races
among whom I was living in Hawaii. When my professor
friend heard that I was engaged to Masahisa, a native of
Japan, he reminded me of what I had said. It's really
amazing what the gospel can do to help one love all
kinds of Japanese—and other people too.

(*Note: Faith Okawa married Masahisa Watabe in the Salt
Lake Temple on December 7, 1965.*)

V
UNTO THE ISLANDS OF THE SEA

22
THE FAITH OF
THE POLYNESIANS

Anthropologists talk of the "Pacific Triangle," a vast region that stretches from New Zealand to Hawaii, from Hawaii to the lonely Easter Island off the coast of Chile, and from Easter Island back across the South Pacific to New Zealand again. Inhabiting these far-flung islands are a people who have undying zest for adventure and extraordinary qualities of simple faith. These are the people of Polynesia—the Hawaiians, Maoris, Tahitians, Samoans, Fijians, and Tongans.

These are the people of whom the late Elder Matthew Cowley of the Council of the Twelve spoke so lovingly and reverently, after spending many years living among them. His report on the Polynesians delivered in general conference in October 1948 is typical of his experiences among these faithful Saints. He told of a couple in Tonga who had been childless for twenty-seven years and who sought a blessing from the hands of the priesthood. Within a year they had been blessed with a child. He told of a Samoan member suffering from elephantiasis who was cured through his faith. He told of being asked by a couple in New Zealand to give their child a name. Then they added, "While you are giving it a name, please give it its vision. It was born blind." "I was overwhelmed," Elder Cowley recalled. "I was doubtful, but I knew that within the being of that Polynesian there was the simple faith of a child, a faith not beclouded by psychology or any of the learning of men, but a simple faith in God and the promises he had made through his Son Jesus Christ. I gave that child its name, and eventually I mustered up enough courage to bless it with its vision." Some six or seven years later Elder Cowley again visited that community, where he saw the little boy to whom he had given the blessing, and, he reported, "he can see as well as I can see this day." ("Among the Polynesians," *Improvement Era,* November 1948, pp. 699f.)

Unique among the Polynesian islands of the Pacific, and one of the smallest kingdoms in the world, is Tonga. In many ways, Tonga is, and has always been, a little world in itself. It has been a British protectorate since the beginning of this century; it has been strongly influenced by the Wesleyan Methodists since the establishment of their mission in 1826; but it is a country whose sovereignty today is Tongan, for its king does command power.

Tonga is made up of some 150 islands whose total land space is approximately half that of the city of Los Angeles, spread out in the South Pacific over eight degrees of latitude and four of longitude. For neighbors, there is Fiji to the west, and Samoa to the north. Tonga is an agricultural country whose inhabitants grow and harvest sugar cane, kava, coconuts (copra), taro, and bananas, the principal cash export crop.

The first Mormon missionaries visited the island kingdom in 1891, and they were cordially received. Since that time Mormon influence in this distinctive country has become remarkably strong. Out of a native population of approximately 90,000 at the end of 1976, some 15,000 were members of The Church of Jesus Christ of Latter-day Saints.

One of these members is Vaha'i Tonga, known on

the records of the Church as Semisi Nukumovaha'i Tonga. His personal story provides a revealing glimpse into the attitudes of simple trust, faith, and prayer that characterize so many of the people of the islands of the Pacific.

When Vaha'i and his older brother, Semisi Motolalo Tonga, were baptized on the seashore of Tonga-tapu on April 6, 1930, none of their relatives knew they were doing so. And there was some shock when they later told them what they had done. Vaha'i was twelve years old, but even then he displayed an uncanny capacity to stand up and be heard.

An elderly, white-haired Tongan, Than Siole Kongaika, clothed impressively in native dress, blessed the water and opened the service. Young Vaha'i was deeply moved that the rushing, incoming waves would always separate and miss this man as he stood on the shore. To Vaha'i this was the first in a lifetime of miracles, his first testimony of the power of the priesthood among the peoples of Polynesia.

As a young man, Vaha'i Tonga was a good student, a person without guile and of implicit courage and faith. He was not afraid to lead. While attending the Government Tonga College in February 1933, he was the only Mormon boy out of four hundred students. On the first Sunday there, when time for chapel arrived, he stood alone under a sign for Mormons; and almost happily he received the taunts of his classmates. Even then he believed that Mormons must be different.

Another incident in his days as a student bears out his record of simple faith. In 1935 he and his classmates visited Mataki'eua plantation on a copra-cutting work project. At about two o'clock in the afternoon it began to rain heavily, so the students were excused to return to their sleeping quarters. About four o'clock the senior tutor, Sione Palei Tu'ipulotu, approached the boys and asked, "Who would like to volunteer to go out in the rain and get Kauri, the college horse, who is lost?" The horse was needed to pull the cart when the roads became too muddy to travel any other way. Nobody else volunteered, so Vaha'i raised his hand. The other boys responded, "Well, look at the Mormon boy." Vaha'i recalls, "That was a challenge for me. I found the horse running with other horses. I chased around a paddock about a half-mile square. And the rain was still pouring down. I was almost frozen to death with the cold. But I remembered what my Sunday School teacher told me when I first converted to the truth: 'If you have problems, kneel down and pray to your Heavenly Father.' So I did. I knelt down by a wet banana tree and offered a prayer: 'Father in Heaven, stop the horse for me.' I felt the horse could now be my teacher; he could show by his actions that the Church is true. When I opened my eyes I found all the horses standing nearby, on a small hill, about fifty yards from me. I went straight to them. None of them moved. It was now dark, and I was drenched. I placed the rope around Kauri's neck and rode back to my teacher. As I returned I could see that there was something of admiration in the hearts of my classmates toward my faith and my church. I cannot forget what the teacher said: 'You are a brave boy. I want the boys in this school to watch you and follow your conduct.' "

And that's the way it has been for Vaha'i Tonga over the years. In August 1938, after he had been in the school five years, the principal composed a testimonial in which he declared that Vaha'i was "a special student in the school"; because of his "honesty, obedience, cleanliness, and faithfulness to his religion, his influence will remain and be remembered."

Honoring the priesthood and always being obedient to the Lord and his servants—these were motivating influences behind the major decisions of Vaha'i's life. They figured prominently in his decision to marry in 1941. His mission president, Emil C. Dunn, told him he should marry, so he started looking for the right young woman. He was concerned with obeying the will of the mission president. In answer to prayer, he decided on Friday night to marry Sela, a young woman who was betrothed to marry another man the following Thursday. He asked her to marry him. On Monday he received a letter from her saying yes, she would marry him, even without her parents' permission. Vaha'i replied: "I will come and talk with your parents. We must marry only in a proper way. I am a priest in the priesthood of God. Our marriage must be honorable." Vaha'i visited Sela's house on Tuesday morning. About forty people were there busily preparing for Thursday's wedding. Sela told them all in words of peacefulness and sweetness, "Please listen to Vaha'i. I love Vaha'i, and I wish to marry with Vaha'i; he is my choice." The people were touched in their hearts, and Vaha'i and Sela, his sweetheart, were married on Wednesday, October 19, 1941. "It was a humbling spiritual experience," he says. "I had honored my priesthood."

In 1943 Vaha'i decided to accept the position as principal of the government school on Niuafo'ou or "Tin Can" Island, as it is known in Tonga. He accepted the post at the urging of the mission president, whom he trusted, believing that the president's word was the will of the Lord for him.

Vaha'i has held many responsible Church positions among the peoples of the Pacific islands. He has served as a labor missionary; a school teacher without pay at Liahona High School; a worker in the New Zealand Temple for two years; and a member of the YWMIA mission board for seventeen years. He was the first Tongan to become a counselor to a mission president.

Vaha'i Tonga's personal story, as recounted in the following pages, is based primarily upon an interview conducted by R. Lanier Britsch at Hamilton, New Zealand, on January 22, 1974, with additional incidents and details obtained by the author through subsequent correspondence.

23

VAHA'I TONGA IS PRAYING NOW

My name is Vaha'i Tonga. I was born on January 22, 1918, in Ha'afeva, Ha'apai, Tonga. My father's name is Tevita Tonga and my mother's name is Lu'isa Fifita 'Okusi. I will never forget the very interesting stories my mother told me about how as a young lady she loved my father very much and wanted to marry him because he was a handsome man with a good singing voice.

I was second in a family of seven boys. My father passed away when I was eight years old, so our family moved to the main island of Tonga-tapu. That was a very sad experience for me. I lived with my mother and members of her family. We belonged to the Methodist Church at that time.

One of my uncles, John Filipe, was a member of the Mormon Church. He took me to a Mormon Primary, and in 1929 and 1930 my teacher was Fred W. Stone. Brother Stone also taught us scouting on Monday nights. It was very interesting because he taught us how to tie knots, how to play games, and also to love birds and animals, and to be obedient to our parents. But when my uncle and his wife were called away on missions for the Church in 1931, my grandfather and grandmother took me back to the government's primary school. They didn't like the Mormon religion.

There was a Mormon chapel near where we lived. One day some of my boy friends invited me to Sunday School there. I decided to go. I was really impressed with the teacher; I loved her lessons, and I knew she was interested in us. My grandparents didn't know I was attending church on Sundays. I would listen to the lessons, then run home before closing exercises, because I knew that if they should learn that I was attending the Mormon Church, they would be angry with me. I would hurry home and start preparing our food in our Tongan oven. When they came back from attending their church they would see that everything was in order and would say, "Oh, wonderful, Brother Tonga! Wonderful Vaha'i! You do a marvelous work."

In early 1930 I started asking them, "Can I become a member of the Mormon Church?" Fortunately, my uncle was a member of the Church and he said I should join. So I told my oldest brother, "Let's go. Let's get baptized." He said, "Yes, let's do it." I knew that he really didn't understand what it meant. But we were baptized into the Church by Ralph D. Olson on April 6, 1930.

After the service we returned home. Our family was outside. I knew they were talking about us. We were really scared. We were expecting them to punish us. As we came near to them I remember that I had a strong feeling to step forward and announce, "We were baptized today in The Church of Jesus Christ of Latter-day Saints." They answered, "Okay, you go ahead. From today you are a member of that church. We want you to keep faithful." And since that time we have remained active in the Church.

In the early years of the 1930s I attended a government school known as Tonga College. I was the only Mormon boy in that school. Do you know, I was really blessed. I felt bold and strong. I would stand and tell them freely, "I'm a Mormon boy. I haven't tasted a cigarette and I haven't tasted liquor."

The most wonderful example in my life at that time was my Sunday School teacher, Hola Tuliakiono. When I was thirteen she had a powerful influence on me. I remember her teaching us about prayer and especially family prayer.

I remember the first night I slept at the school with my roommates. I knelt down and tried to say a prayer before going to sleep. My roommate stood right next to me while I was praying and called out: "Look and listen. Here is Joseph Smith. He's praying now!"

My schoolmates did not pray, and it was always noisy in our sleeping rooms when I tried to. But I decided to keep trying. The boy who had yelled and made fun of me was later the first one to kneel down with me in prayer. The second week he sat on his bed and as I was praying he called out to the other boys, "Quiet. Vaha'i Tonga is praying now." Finally all of them began to be quiet at prayer time. Later they knelt down and joined me in family prayer.

I remembered also how scared I was the first year I attended Tonga College at age thirteen. I remembered the branch president asking us boys, "How many hours have you spent doing priesthood work?" So I decided to work at the Church on Saturday afternoons. I went alone into the chapel and straightened chairs, swept the floor, and picked up rubbish. While I was there one day the mission president, Emil Dunn, saw me working and asked, "Where are you from?"

I said, "From Tonga College."

"Well, why do you come over here to do this work?"

"I am a deacon, aren't I?"

And he said, "That's okay."

So I worked with him cleaning the yards.

At about six o'clock he gave me a loaf of bread and a pound of corned beef. I needed it very badly. I had no home to live in at that time, and many times I didn't have enough food to eat. Besides that, I loved to work in the chapel. Also, from then on I knew the president would give me bread and meat when I worked on Saturdays. So I never missed a Saturday.

One day President Dunn's wife said, "Brother Tonga, we want to help you." They began to treat me like a son. I will never forget that in all my life.

After I started to work hard on Saturdays at the Church, many of the young people started joining me. I would invite them. And I was thankful as they began coming. President Dunn said, "Any time you need help, please come to me." And I went to him sometimes when I felt hungry. But I never asked for food unless I worked for it. When I had free time at school I would go to the Church and water the plants and pick up rubbish. Sometimes Sister Dunn would leave cookies for me.

I remember my first experience at a district conference. I told some of my friends we were going to have district conference the coming Sunday. They wanted to go with me. I said, "Sure, you can attend." I went around like a missionary inviting people to go with me. The school said we could go if we signed a paper. Seventy-seven signed up. When I gave the paper to the principal, he called out the names and asked, "Are all of you members of the Mormon Church?" I stood up and said, "Yes, sir." "Okay." He signed his approval. "Today is Friday. After four o'clock you may leave and come back on Monday morning." I took seventy-seven of my friends to district conference. It was fun for them to go free from school. We joined in sports competition at the conference. We won the competition in rugby and tennis. They all loved it. We baptized seven young people at that district conference.

Another morning the principal stood up in school and asked, "Where's Tonga?" I raised my hand. Then he said, "Today we will call the Mormon boy to be our prefect. He is trustworthy and I am proud of him." From that time on nobody teased me about Joseph Smith, not even my teachers.

When I first joined the Church many young people at school used to make fun of my religion by asking me how many wives I had. But now as I look around in

Tonga I can see many of these same people who are
faithful members of the Church.

After five years at Tonga College I went on my first
mission. I had already married and the government
called me to be principal and director of education on
the northern island of "Tin Can." They said, "We'll call
the Mormon boy because he's dependable." But I told
them, "No, I won't go." I did not want to accept the job
because there were no members of the Church on the
island. But as it turned out, the mission president came
to me that same day and said, "Brother Tonga, the Lord
has called you to go on a mission to Tin Can Island. Can
you accept this call?" I answered immediately, "Yes, sir.
I will go." The mission president explained that I could
be a missionary and also be a teacher for the government
there. He told me to go over to the director and tell him
that I had decided to accept the appointment. The
mission president also cautioned me: "In this new job,
don't talk about the Church until after at least three
months. This way the people will not get upset, and you
will avoid a lot of trouble with the government. Just go
there and be careful. Listen to the people and see if they
want to hear about the Church."

I arrived at Tin Can Island on Thursday evening.
Two of my former roommates were living there. They
said, "Look out, here comes a Mormon missionary."
They introduced me as I walked in, and asked, "Can you
talk to the people here? We would like to hear about the
Mormons." I had been instructed by my mission
president to wait three months. He had also told me that
it would take six months before we could think of
organizing a branch or a ward. But these two friends
had already told the local people that I was a Mormon
missionary. They had already said, "If you want to
listen, he's got a really fantastic church."

So I held my first cottage meeting that Friday night
and I shall never forget it. I talked at least for an hour. I
would sing songs, then talk for about ten minutes, and
sing more songs, and talk some more. I learned that on
the island there was an inactive member of the Church

who had been there five years. He had become an important man in the Methodist Church. He was a teacher in the government school. He taught music and songs, including the hymns of his church. He was also teaching principles of the gospel to the people. Through him it seemed the Lord was preparing the way for me. Because of him, it was easier for me to preach the gospel to the people. I was twenty-five years of age at the time.

I started teaching the gospel to the people from that very first night. I notified the mission president that I was sorry, but I could not wait three months. On Monday morning I received a telegram from him that said, "Brother Tonga, this is fine. According to what I feel from the Spirit, if you are willing to move forward now, do so." This was the happiest moment of my life. After the first month we had organized a Sunday School and baptized five people. I felt very, very humble. And very grateful.

I spent three years on that island. I was really pleased at the end of the first year when the government director of education and one of his assistants came to inspect my school. Inspections are always difficult. My school was rated as the second best school in the kingdom. I received a letter of congratulations from the officials. Also, some of my friends and fellow teachers wrote and said, "Mr. Tonga, you must be very up in the air. How did you do it? How did you become such a successful teacher so soon?" Well, I knew. I knew it was because I was a priesthood holder. And I remembered the mission president's instructions; "If you live close to our Father in heaven, you will succeed."

In three years' time there were seven Mormon missionaries assigned to Tin Can Island. We had built up a branch of about thirty-four members.

After I returned home I was called to serve as a labor missionary for two years, from 1948 to 1950. I was teaching and also helping to build a school. I had four children at the time. After completing calls to serve on three missions for the Church, I was appointed as a government inspector of schools.

We went to the temple in New Zealand for the first time in 1958. It had been announced that the temple would be dedicated, and there was much discussion about who would like to attend that dedication. I made it clear that I would like to attend with my wife, Sela. This was on a Tuesday. Fred Stone, mission president at the time, was a tremendous person. He had been my teacher when I was nine years old. He's still my teacher. I was able to talk to him about anything. On Tuesday evening he and his wife came to our house, and he said, "Brother Tonga, I want you to get all the money you have saved to go to the temple and bring it over to me. We need it to help build a chapel in your branch. If we don't do it now the building program will pass by your branch, and you will have to wait a couple of years to get approval for it to be built. Can you do that, Brother Tonga?"

I said, "President, I'll do it. Tomorrow I'll get the money." I talked with my wife and she said, "We'll do it."

I had already told some of my friends and family that we were going to the dedication of the temple. Now I said to my wife, "Let's close the door to Satan in our lives. Let's do what the Lord wants us to do."

Wednesday morning I went over to the government bank and drew out all of the money. I gave it to my wife and told her to give it to President Stone. That night we had a little talk. I said, "Honey, the Lord has promised us through our leaders that if we keep his commandments he will prepare some way that we will be able to go to the dedication. We have cows, pigs, and some horses, besides furniture and mats. Let's sell them all so we may be able to receive the blessings of the dedication."

We began to tell people that we wanted to sell our livestock, but when they came to see it they said, "No, too much money. Too dear for us to buy those things." This was on Thursday, and Friday was not successful either. On the following Monday the ship, the *Tofua*, was to leave.

On Saturday morning three families came who needed some cows, pigs, and other things, and we received an equivalent of between $500 and $600 in about half an hour. I told my wife that we had the money and would be able to go. I went over early Monday morning to Nuku'alofa to give President Stone the money. In surprise he asked, "Where did you get the money?"

"We sold some of our things so that we may go to the dedication."

"Brother Tonga," he said, "the Lord will bless you."

At the temple we realized many blessings. We were the first witness couple and the first couple to be sealed in the New Zealand Temple. I was the leader of the Tongan chorus, and President McKay asked me to lead the entire congregation in the closing hymn of the dedicatory service.

When my wife and I were sealed to each other, something touched my heart. Our children were not with us, and tears came to my eyes. When we arrived home I promised our four children that if they would help, we could all go to the temple together. I thought to myself, "How can you say, be a good boy or be a good girl, if you are not sealed to them in the temple." I had the feeling that they were not mine.

For two years we sacrificed almost everything. I divided my pay from school for each one of us, and we saved that. After we paid our tithing and fast offerings, we were left with seventy cents in our hands each month. This is how our family lived for two years, on seventy cents a month. We lived on what we could grow and gather. My wife would wake up early in the morning to make our salads with bananas and coconut milk. My children could not buy candy or shoes or go to movies because they were saving to go to the temple.

In addition to my regular teaching job at Liahona High School, I did some other work as it came along. To save on transportation costs, I rode my bicycle to district meetings in Nuku'alofa, seven miles away. I was a counselor to the president of the mission YMMIA and had to travel from branch to branch. I rode my bike on these assignments. Most of our district meetings began at six o'clock in the morning, so I had to leave home very early. When the deadline came for getting our money in, my five-year-old daughter, Tapata, said, "Dad, let me go and count my money." She counted it and said, "I'm through, I've got enough money to go to the temple." The two oldest girls, Leslieli Fipe and Mafi, said they had about $235. After saving for two years the little one, Lihai, had saved $65. I had saved almost $1,300 for my family.

Through sacrifice we were able to take our family to New Zealand to be sealed in the temple. We had to do some extra things in order to accomplish our goals, but it was a great blessing to us.

INDEX